Dr Michael M. Gruneberg, designer and writer Gruneberg Linkword Language Course, is widely acknowledged as an international expert on memory improvement. A Senior Lecturer in Psychology at University College, Swansea, he has published a large number of articles in scientific journals, as well as a number of well-known books on the application of memory research. He has also lectured widely in both the UK and the USA and addressed several international scientific conferences. In 1988 he provided the original script for and appeared in *The Magic of Memory*, a programme in the BBC television QED series which illustrated many memory techniques, including his own Linkword Method.

The Linkword Courses have grown out of a large body of published scientific research showing that the imagery method they employ is highly effective in improving the memory for foreign language vocabulary. One study has shown that using method increases retention from 28% to 88% for a list of 60 Spanish words. Dr Gruneberg has taken this work considerably further, working with linguists and setting out images and testing patterns to create a fully-integrated language-learning system capable of teaching both vocabulary and grammar.

Since it was first published in 1987, the Linkword system has been both highly successful and widely acclaimed.

Gabriel C. Jacobs BA, PhD, the language consultant for this book, is a Lecturer in Romance Studies at the University College of Swansea. He has been involved for some time in the practical application of language.

'We have found the Linkword programmes to be both effective and entertaining'
Brian Ablett, Training Development Officer, British Caledonian

'Feel free to quote me as a satisfied customer'
Michael Woodhall, Director Language Learning Centre, Manchester Business School

'It took me 12 hours to teach a regime that normally takes 40 hours'
Peter Marsh, Thomson Holidays

'I was frankly astounded at how effective this visual imagery was as an aid to memory retention'
Lolita Taylor, Popular Computer World

'I tried the system out in both German and French and was amazed at how quickly it worked'
Jan McCann, Toronto Sun

'I learned German vocabulary at about twice the speed . . . If you want to learn or brush up on a foreign language, this system will accelerate your learning beyond anything you have experienced in conventional foreign-language instruction'
Professor Douglas J. Herrman, Applied Cognitive Psychology

Also by Dr Michael Gruneberg

and published by Corgi Books

LINKWORD
LANGUAGE SYSTEM

SPANISH

Dr Michael M. Gruneberg

Language Consultant
Gabriel C. Jacobs

CORGI BOOKS

To John Beloff

LINKWORD LANGUAGE SYSTEM – SPANISH
A CORGI BOOK 0 552 13055 9

First publication in Great Britain

PRINTING HISTORY
Corgi edition published 1987
Corgi edition reprinted 1988 (twice)
Corgi edition reprinted 1989
Corgi edition reissued 1991
Corgi edition reprinted 1992
Corgi edition reprinted 1993
Corgi edition reprinted 1994

This book is set in 9/10pt Century
by Colset Private Limited, Singapore

Corgi Books are published by Transworld Publishers Ltd,
61– 63 Uxbridge Road, Ealing, London W5 5SA,
in Australia by Transworld Publishers (Australia) Pty Ltd,
15– 25 Helles Avenue, Moorebank, NSW 2170,
and in New Zealand by Transworld Publishers (NZ) Ltd,
3 William Pickering Drive, Albany, Auckland.

Printed and bound in Great Britain by
Cox & Wyman Ltd, Reading, Berkshire

Contents

A Foreword by Paul Daniels

As you may know I, Paul Daniels, am a professional magician, and as such am involved in the business of deception. I am also writing this foreword without ever having seen the full text of this book.

Add these two facts together and you may well wonder why or how I can speak with any degree of authority or expect to be believed when I extol the virtues of the Linkword system.

Well, the simple truth is that one Monday morning at nine a.m. I did not speak a single word of Spanish and by five p.m. on the following Friday I knew hundreds of words of Spanish! I know that is true because I counted them!! Please note the use of the word 'knew' in the last sentence . . . it was chosen deliberately . . . I knew the words positively enough to KNOW that when I said them they were the correct words. My brain reeled with the excitement of learning so much so fast. At forty-eight years of age I had finally got to the stage of being able to communicate with people of another language . . . and how they loved me for trying.

A few weeks later, with no more lessons other than my own reading of Spanish newspapers and books I went on stage and performed my act entirely in Spanish, and now I am 'all fired up' and anxious to learn more. It's wonderful.

Memory systems go back a long way, and I have read many that have suggested their methods could be applied to language learning, but this system is the first I have come across where someone has actually provided a complete system that is 'ready to go'. When you first read memory systems that use idiotic association as a memory aid it is very easy to think that the idea itself is stupid, BUT IT WORKS!!!

So, do yourself a favour and don't knock it till you have tried it. Once you have found out for yourself how to use your own imagination fully to really 'see' the mental images I am sure that like me you will be wondering why this 'game' of learning language is not taught in all our schools.

Paul Daniels

INTRODUCTION

TEST YOURSELF WITH LINKWORD

Picture each of these images in your mind's eye for about ten seconds. For example, the French for *tablecloth* is *nappe*. Imagine yourself having a nap on a tablecloth, as vividly as you can, for about ten seconds.

- The French for TABLECLOTH is NAPPE
  Imagine having a *NAP* on a *TABLECLOTH*.

- The German for GENTLEMEN is HERREN
  Imagine a *HERRING* dangling from the door of a *GENTLEMEN'S* toilet.

- The Italian for FLY is MOSCA.
  Imagine *FLIES* invading *MOSCOW*.

- The Spanish for SUITCASE is MALETA
  Imagine *MY LETTER* in your *SUITCASE*.

- The French for HEDGEHOG is HERISSON.
  Imagine your *HAIRY SON* looks like a *HEDGEHOG*.

- The German for LETTER is BRIEF.
  Imagine a *BRIEF LETTER*.

- The Italian for DRAWER is CASSETTO.
  Imagine you keep *CASSETTES* in a *DRAWER*.

- The Spanish for WAITRESS is CAMARERA.
  Imagine a *WAITRESS* with a *CAMERA* slung around her neck!

NOW TURN OVER

○ What is the English for CAMARERA? _____

○ What is the English for CASSETTO? _____

○ What is the English for BRIEF? _____

○ What is the English for HERISSON? _____

○ What is the English for MALETA? _____

○ What is the English for MOSCA? _____

○ What is the English for HERREN? _____

○ What is the English for NAPPE? _____

TURN BACK FOR THE ANSWERS.

Do not expect to get them all correct at the first attempt. However, if you feel you got more right than you normally would have — then this course will suit you!

WHO IS LINKWORD FOR?

The short answer is that Linkword is for anyone and everyone who wants to learn the basics of a language in a hurry. It can be used by children or by adults. Even young children who cannot read can be taught Spanish words by a parent reading out the images.

The Linkword Courses have been carefully designed to teach you a basic grammar and words in a simple step-by-step way that anyone can follow. After about 10—12 hours, or even less, you will have a vocabulary of literally hundreds of words and the ability to string these words together to form sentences. The course is ideal, therefore, for the holidaymaker or business person who just wants the basics in a hurry so he or she can be understood, e.g. in the hotel, arriving at the destination, sightseeing, eating out, in emergencies, telling the time and so on.

The course is also an ideal supplement to schoolwork. Many school pupils feel that they remember words for the first time when introduced to the Linkword system, and understood basic grammar for the first time too!

HOW TO USE LINKWORD

1] You will be presented with words like this:
   The Spanish for CAT is GATO
   Imagine a CAT eating a lovely GATEAU
   What you do is to imagine this picture in your mind's eye as vividly as possible.

2] After you have read the image you should think about it in your mind's eye for about 10 seconds before moving on to the next word. If you do not spend enough time thinking about the image it will not stick in your memory as well as it should.

3] Sometimes the word in Spanish and in English is the same or very similar. For example, the Spanish for "taxi" is "taxi". When this happens you will be asked to associate the word in some way with a bullfighter.

   Imagine a taxi filled with bullfighters. Whenever bullfighters come to mind, therefore, you will know the word is the same or similar in both English and Spanish.

4] The examples given in the course may well strike you as silly and bizarre. They have deliberately been given in this way to show up points of grammar and to get away from the idea that you should remember useful phrases "parrot fashion".

5] ACCENTS

When you see this accent Ñ you should pronounce it ENYER
For example: The Spanish for TOMORROW is MAÑANA
MANYANA is the way the word is pronounced.

When you see an acute accent (´) on a vowel you should emphasise
the syllable with the accented vowel in it.
For example: The Spanish for MOUSE is RATÓN
RAT *ON* is the way the word is pronounced (*not RAT
ON*)

6] PRONUNCIATION

The approximate pronunciation of words is given in brackets
after the word is presented for the first time.
For example: The Spanish for COW is VACA (VAKA)
(VAKA) is the way the word is pronounced.

Do not worry too much about these pronunciations to begin with.
The approximate pronunciation given in brackets will allow you to
be understood. If you would like to listen to the exact pronunciation,
an audio-tape containing all the words on the course is available
from Corgi Books.

SOME USEFUL HINTS

1. It is usually best to go through the course as quickly as possible. Many people can get through most of the course in a weekend, especially if they start on Friday evening.

2. Take a break of about 10 minutes between each section, and always *stop* if you feel tired.

3. Don't worry about forgetting a few words, and do not go back to relearn words you have forgotten. Just think of how much you are learning, and try to pick up the forgotten words when it comes to revising.

4. Revise after Section 4, Section 8 and at the end of the course. Then revise the whole course a week later and a month later.

5. Don't worry if you forget some of the words or grammar after a time. Relearning is extremely fast, and going through the book for a few hours just before you go abroad will quickly get you back to where you were.

6. The course will not give you conversational fluency. You can't expect this until you go abroad and live in a country for a period of time. What it will give you very rapidly is the ability to survive in a large number of situations you will meet abroad. Once you have got this framework, you will find it much easier to pick up more words and grammar when you travel.

IMPORTANT NOTE

**The first section of the course can be basically regarded as a
training section designed to get you into the Linkword
method quickly and easily.**

After about 45 minutes you will have a vocabulary of about 30
words and be able to translate sentences. Once you have finished
Section 1 you will have the confidence to go through the rest of the
course just as quickly. Animal words are used in the first section as
they are a large group of "easy to image" words. Many animal words
of course are useful to have as they are often met abroad, e.g. dog,
cat, etc., or they are edible!

Finally, when it comes to translating sentences the answers are
given at the foot of the page. You may find it useful to cover up the
answers before you tackle the translations.

Section 1 ANIMALS

N.B. The word on the right-hand side of the page (IN BRACKETS) is the way the word is pronounced.

THINK OF EACH IMAGE IN YOUR MIND'S EYE FOR ABOUT TEN SECONDS

○ The Spanish for CAT is GATO　　　　　　　　　(GATO)
　Imagine you GET TO hold a lovely cat.

○ The Spanish for DOG is PERRO　　　　　　　　(PERRO)
　Imagine a dog PIROUETTING.

○ The Spanish for GOAT is CABRA　　　　　　　(KABRA)
　Imagine a COBRA striking at a goat.

○ The Spanish for BULL is TORO　　　　　　　　(TORO)
　Imagine a TOREADOR fighting a bull.

○ The Spanish for COW is VACA　　　　　　　　(VAKA)
　Imagine a cow with a VACUUM cleaner
　cleaning the field.

○ The Spanish for DUCK is PATO　　　　　　　　(PATO)
　Imagine PATTING a duck on its head, or
　imagine duck pate.

○ The Spanish for GOOSE is GANSO　　　　　　(GANSO)
　Imagine GANGS OF geese going around together.

○ The Spanish for PIG is PUERCO　　　　　　(POO ERKO)
　Imagine eating PORK straight from a pig.

○ The Spanish for DONKEY is BURRO　　　　　(BOORRO)
　Imagine a donkey at a writing BUREAU.

○ The Spanish for FROG is RANA　　　　　　　　(RANA)
　Imagine you RAN A mile after seeing a horrible frog.

YOU CAN WRITE YOUR ANSWERS IN

○ What is the English for rana?   _____

○ What is the English for burro?   _____

○ What is the English for puerco?   _____

○ What is the English for ganso?   _____

○ What is the English for pato?   _____

○ What is the English for vaca?   _____

○ What is the English for toro?   _____

○ What is the English for cabra?   _____

○ What is the English for perro?   _____

○ What is the English for gato?   _____

TURN BACK FOR THE ANSWERS

COVER UP THE LEFT HAND PAGE BEFORE ANSWERING

○ What is the Spanish for frog? _____

○ What is the Spanish for donkey? _____

○ What is the Spanish for pig? _____

○ What is the Spanish for goose? _____

○ What is the Spanish for duck? _____

○ What is the Spanish for cow? _____

○ What is the Spanish for bull? _____

○ What is the Spanish for goat? _____

○ What is the Spanish for dog? _____

○ What is the Spanish for cat? _____

TURN BACK FOR THE ANSWERS

ELEMENTARY GRAMMAR

The first bit of grammar to learn is that all nouns, or things, whether living or non-living, are either masculine or feminine. If they end in an "o", they are masculine.

For example,

BULL is TORO, CAT is GATO and DOG is PERRO. All these words end in an "o" and are therefore masculine words.

Words which end in an "a" are feminine words. CABRA for GOAT and VACA for COW end in an "a" and are therefore feminine words.

What are the genders of:

VACA

PATO

BURRO

RANA

GANSO

The answers are:

VACA is FEMININE

PATO is MASCULINE

BURRO is MASCULINE

RANA is FEMININE

GANSO is MASCULINE

A few words do not end in "o" or "a". Do not worry about these. We will deal with them later.

MORE ANIMALS

THINK OF EACH IMAGE IN YOUR MIND'S EYE FOR ABOUT TEN SECONDS

○ The Spanish for MONKEY is MONO   (MONO)
Imagine a monkey wearing a MONOCLE.

○ The Spanish for RAT is RATA   (RATA)
Imagine a RAT fighting a bullfighter.

○ The Spanish for MOUSE is RATÓN   (RATON)
Imagine a RAT ON a mouse, squashing it flat.

○ The Spanish for ANIMAL is ANIMAL   (ANEEMAL)
Imagine a bullfighter surrounded by a whole
lot of different ANIMALS.

○ The Spanish for SALMON is SALMÓN   (SALMON)
Imagine a SALMON leaping over a bullfighter.

○ The Spanish for WASP is AVISPA   (AVEESPA)
Imagine A WHISPER in your ear as a wasp
buzzes near you.

○ The Spanish for BEAR is OSO   (OSO)
Imagine a big grizzly bear OH! SO near you.

○ The Spanish for A (LIVE) FISH is PEZ   (PETH)
Imagine a fish in an aquarium eating the
PITH of an orange.

○ The Spanish for ELEPHANT is   (ELEFANTAY)
ELEFANTE
Imagine a bullfighter fighting an ELEPHANT.

○ The Spanish for BEE is ABEJA   (ABEHA)
Imagine A BAKER being chased by a bee.

YOU CAN WRITE YOUR ANSWERS IN

○ What is the English for abeja?   _____

○ What is the English for elefante?   _____

○ What is the English for pez?   _____

○ What is the English for oso?   _____

○ What is the English for avispa?   _____

○ What is the English for salmón?   _____

○ What is the English for animal?   _____

○ What is the English for ratón?   _____

○ What is the English for rata?   _____

○ What is the English for mono?   _____

TURN BACK FOR THE ANSWERS

COVER UP THE LEFT HAND PAGE BEFORE ANSWERING

○ What is the Spanish for bee?   _____

○ What is the Spanish for elephant?   _____

○ What is the Spanish for fish?   _____

○ What is the Spanish for bear?   _____

○ What is the Spanish for wasp?   _____

○ What is the Spanish for salmon?   _____

○ What is the Spanish for animal?   _____

○ What is the Spanish for mouse?   _____

○ What is the Spanish for rat?   _____

○ What is the Spanish for monkey?   _____

TURN BACK FOR THE ANSWERS

ELEMENTARY GRAMMAR

You learned after the last group of words that all nouns are either masculine or feminine. If they end in "o" they are masculine, like GATO for CAT. If they end in "a" they are feminine like CABRA for GOAT.

If they do not end in either an "o" or an "a", you can assume they are masculine, although you will make the occasional mistake.

If the word is MASCULINE, then the word for THE is EL.

So, EL TORO is THE BULL

   EL GATO is THE CAT

   EL MONO is THE MONKEY

Try to remember that men are HELL to live with.

If the word is FEMININE, however, then the word for THE is LA.

So, LA VACA   is THE COW

   LA RATA   is THE RAT

   LA CABRA   is THE GOAT

As we saw just now, where the word does not end in an "a" or an "o", such as ANIMAL, RATÓN, PEZ, etc., it is almost always masculine.

So, EL ANIMAL   is THE ANIMAL

   EL PEZ   is THE FISH

   EL ELEFANTE is THE ELEPHANT

Now cover up the answers below and translate the following:

THE DOG
THE SALMON
THE GOAT
THE COW
THE BEE
THE WASP
THE MOUSE
THE ANIMAL
THE DONKEY
THE DUCK
THE FROG
THE BEAR

The answers are:

EL PERRO
EL SALMÓN
LA CABRA
LA VACA
LA ABEJA
LA AVISPA
EL RATÓN
EL ANIMAL
EL BURRO
EL PATO
LA RANA
EL OSO

SOME ADJECTIVES (DESCRIPTIVE WORDS)

THINK OF EACH IMAGE IN YOUR MIND'S EYE FOR ABOUT TEN SECONDS

○ The Spanish for HARD is DURO   (DOORO)
   Imagine something HARD and DURABLE.

○ The Spanish for QUICK is RÁPIDO   (RAPEEDO)
   Imagine something RAPID and QUICK.

○ The Spanish for QUIET is TRANQUILO   (TRANKEELO)
   Imagine everything being TRANQUIL and QUIET.

○ The Spanish for FRESH is FRESCO   (FRESKO)
   Imagine seeing a FRESCO FRESHLY
   painted on a wall.

○ The Spanish for GOOD is BUENO   (BOO ENO)
   Imagine there must be something GOOD in BUENOs Aires!

○ The Spanish for BAD is MALO   (MALO)
   Imagine a BAD marshMALLOW.

YOU CAN WRITE YOUR ANSWERS IN

○ What is the English for malo? _____

○ What is the English for bueno? _____

○ What is the English for fresco? _____

○ What is the English for tranquilo? _____

○ What is the English for rápido? _____

○ What is the English for duro? _____

TURN BACK FOR THE ANSWERS

COVER UP THE LEFT HAND PAGE BEFORE ANSWERING

○ What is the Spanish for bad? _____

○ What is the Spanish for good? _____

○ What is the Spanish for fresh? _____

○ What is the Spanish for quiet? _____

○ What is the Spanish for quick? _____

○ What is the Spanish for hard? _____

TURN BACK FOR THE ANSWERS

ELEMENTARY GRAMMAR

The Spanish word for IS is ESTÁ.

Imagine A STAR is born.

For example:

THE PIG IS   is EL PUERCO ESTÁ
THE DOG IS ·is EL PERRO ESTÁ

To say THE PIG IS QUICK you simply say:

EL PUERCO ESTÁ RÁPIDO
THE DOG IS QUICK is EL PERRO ESTÁ RÁPIDO

If the noun is feminine, such as LA VACA, LA CABRA, and so on, then the ending of the adjective changes to an "a" from an "o" to agree with the noun.

So,

THE COW IS QUICK is LA VACA ESTÁ RÁPIDA
(N.B. not RÁPIDO)

· Similarly,

THE GOAT IS QUICK is LA CABRA ESTÁ RÁPIDA.

Now cover up the answers below and translate the following:

(You can write your answers in)

1. THE DOG IS FRESH
2. THE FISH IS QUICK
3. THE ELEPHANT IS FRESH
4. THE GOAT IS QUIET.
5. THE COW IS QUICK

The answers are:

1. EL PERRO ESTÁ FRESCO
2. EL PEZ ESTÁ RÁPIDO
3. EL ELEFANTE ESTÁ FRESCO
4. LA CABRA ESTÁ TRANQUILA
5. LA VACA ESTÁ RÁPIDA

The other adjectives you have learned can be used in the same way, but exactly how they should be used will be explained in the next section.

Now cover up the answers below and translate the following:

(You can write your answers in)

1. EL ANIMAL ESTÁ FRESCO
2. EL OSO ESTÁ RÁPIDO
3. EL GANSO ESTÁ TRANQUILO
4. EL MONO ESTÁ FRESCO
5. LA AVISPA ESTÁ RÁPIDA

The answers are:

1. THE ANIMAL IS FRESH
2. THE BEAR IS QUICK
3. THE GOOSE IS QUIET
4. THE MONKEY IS FRESH
5. THE WASP IS QUICK

SOME USEFUL ANIMAL WORDS

THINK OF EACH IMAGE IN YOUR MIND'S EYE FOR ABOUT TEN SECONDS

○ The Spanish for BIRD is PÁJARO   (PAHARO)
   Imagine a bird is a PARROT.

○ The Spanish for HORSE is CABALLO   (KABALYO)
   Imagine saying "I'll CABLE YOU if my horse wins."

○ The Spanish for JELLYFISH is MEDUSA   (MEDOOSA)
   Imagine seeing MEDUSA with her head of
   snakes, but when you look carefully it is a jellyfish.

○ The Spanish for FLY is MOSCA   (MOSKA)
   Imagine MOSCOW invaded by a cloud of flies.

○ The Spanish for CHICKEN is POLLO   (POLYO)
   Imagine playing POLO with a chicken instead of a stick.

YOU CAN WRITE YOUR ANSWERS IN

○ What is the English for pollo?   _____

○ What is the English for mosca?   _____

○ What is the English for medusa? _____

○ What is the English for caballo?   _____

○ What is the English for pájaro?   _____

TURN BACK FOR THE ANSWERS

COVER UP THE LEFT HAND PAGE BEFORE ANSWERING

○ What is the Spanish for chicken? _____

○ What is the Spanish for fly? _____

○ What is the Spanish for jellyfish? _____

○ What is the Spanish for horse? _____

○ What is the Spanish for bird? _____

TURN BACK FOR THE ANSWERS

ELEMENTARY GRAMMAR

When you have a noun and an adjective together like HARD PIG, QUIET COW or QUICK BEAR, then the adjective usually comes after the noun.

For example:

THE QUIET BEE   is LA ABEJA TRANQUILA

THE HARD PIG   is EL PUERCO DURO

THE QUICK FROG is LA RANA RÁPIDA

Now cover up the answers below and translate the following:

(You can write your answers in)

1. THE QUICK CAT IS QUIET
2. THE HARD ELEPHANT IS QUICK
3. THE FRESH BIRD IS QUICK
4. THE QUIET JELLYFISH IS QUICK
5. THE QUICK HORSE IS FRESH

The answers are:

1. EL GATO RÁPIDO ESTÁ TRANQUILO
2. EL ELEFANTE DURO ESTÁ RÁPIDO
3. EL PÁJARO FRESCO ESTÁ RÁPIDO
4. LA MEDUSA TRANQUILA ESTÁ RÁPIDA
5. EL CABALLO RÁPIDO ESTÁ FRESCO

Now cover up the answers below and translate the following:

(You can write your answers in)

1. EL POLLO TRANQUILO ESTÁ FRESCO
2. LA RANA FRESCA ESTÁ RÁPIDA
3. LA MOSCA RÁPIDA ESTÁ TRANQUILA
4. EL POLLO FRESCO ESTÁ RÁPIDO
5. LA MEDUSA FRESCA ESTÁ RÁPIDA

The answers are:

1. THE QUIET CHICKEN IS FRESH
2. THE FRESH FROG IS QUICK
3. THE QUICK FLY IS QUIET
4. THE FRESH CHICKEN IS QUICK
5. THE FRESH JELLYFISH IS QUICK

IMPORTANT NOTE

Some of the sentences in this course might strike you as being a bit odd!

However, they have been carefully constructed to make you think much more about what you are translating. This helps the memory process and gets away from the idea of learning useful phrases "parrot fashion".

But of course, having learned with the help of these seemingly odd sentences you can easily construct your own sentences to suit your particular needs.

Section 2   HOTEL/HOME, FURNITURE, COLOURS

FURNITURE AND FITTINGS

THINK OF EACH IMAGE IN YOUR MIND'S EYE FOR ABOUT TEN SECONDS

○ The Spanish for BED is CAMA   (KAMA)
   Imagine a CAMEL lying on your bed.

○ The Spanish for TABLE is MESA   (MESA)
   Imagine a MESSY table.

○ The Spanish for CHAIR is SILLA   (SEELYA)
   Imagine a girl called CELIA sitting down on a large chair.

○ The Spanish for CURTAIN is CORTINA   (KORTEENA)
   Imagine you CONCERTINA your curtains
   when you open them.

○ The Spanish for CUPBOARD is ARMARIO   (ARMARYO)
   Imagine you keep an ARMOURY of weapons
   in your cupboard.

○ The Spanish for MIRROR is ESPEJO   (ESPEHO)
   Imagine looking at A SPECKLED mirror.

○ The Spanish for PIANO is PIANO   (PEE ANO)
   Imagine a bullfighter playing a PIANO.

○ The Spanish for CLOCK is RELOJ   (RELOH)
   Imagine RELOADING a clock.

○ The Spanish for SHELF is ESTANTE   (ESTANTAY)
   Imagine putting up INSTANT shelving.

○ The Spanish for DRAWER is CAJÓN   (KAHON)
   Imagine a CAR HORN sounds every time you
   open your drawer.

YOU CAN WRITE YOUR ANSWERS IN

○ What is the English for cajón? _____

○ What is the English for estante? _____

○ What is the English for reloj? _____

○ What is the English for piano? _____

○ What is the English for espejo? _____

○ What is the English for armario? _____

○ What is the English for cortina? _____

○ What is the English for silla? _____

○ What is the English for mesa? _____

○ What is the English for cama? _____

TURN BACK FOR THE ANSWERS

COVER UP THE LEFT HAND PAGE BEFORE ANSWERING

○ What is the Spanish for drawer? _____

○ What is the Spanish for shelf? _____

○ What is the Spanish for clock? _____

○ What is the Spanish for piano? _____

○ What is the Spanish for mirror? _____

○ What is the Spanish for cupboard? _____

○ What is the Spanish for curtain? _____

○ What is the Spanish for chair? _____

○ What is the Spanish for table? _____

○ What is the Spanish for bed? _____

TURN BACK FOR THE ANSWERS

SOME COLOURS

THINK OF EACH IMAGE IN YOUR MIND'S EYE FOR ABOUT TEN SECONDS

○ The Spanish for COLOUR is COLOR   (KOLOR)
  Imagine a bullfighter with a coat of many COLOURS.

○ The Spanish for BLACK is NEGRO   (NEGRO)
  Imagine a NEGRO, coloured BLACK.

○ The Spanish for WHITE is BLANCO   (BLANKO)
  Imagine a WHITE piece of paper,
  completely BLANK.

○ The Spanish for GREY is GRIS   (GREES)
  Imagine a patch of GREASE on the floor,
  all GREY and horrible.

○ The Spanish for YELLOW is AMARILLO   (AMAREELYO)
  Imagine an ARMADILLO painted all YELLOW.

○ The Spanish for RED IS ROJO   (ROHO)
  Imagine seeing someone who is RED and RAW.

○ The Spanish for GREEN is VERDE   (VERDAY)
  Imagine the composer VERDI, covered in
  GREEN paint.

○ The Spanish for BLUE is AZUL   (ATHUL)
  Imagine tipping a pot of BLUE paint over
  someone who is acting like A FOOL.

YOU CAN WRITE YOUR ANSWERS IN

○ What is the English for azul?   _____

○ What is the English for verde?   _____

○ What is the English for rojo?   _____

○ What is the English for amarillo?   _____

○ What is the English for gris?   _____

○ What is the English for blanco?   _____

○ What is the English for negro?   _____

○ What is the English for color?   _____

TURN BACK FOR THE ANSWERS

COVER UP THE LEFT HAND PAGE BEFORE ANSWERING

○ What is the Spanish for blue? _____

○ What is the Spanish for green? _____

○ What is the Spanish for red? _____

○ What is the Spanish for yellow? _____

○ What is the Spanish for grey? _____

○ What is the Spanish for white? _____

○ What is the Spanish for black? _____

○ What is the Spanish for colour? _____

TURN BACK FOR THE ANSWERS

SOME MORE USEFUL ADJECTIVES

THINK OF EACH IMAGE IN YOUR MIND'S EYE FOR ABOUT TEN SECONDS

○ The Spanish for PRETTY is BONITO   (BONEETO)
Imagine thinking "I have a PRETTY
BONNY TOE."

○ The Spanish for FREE is LIBRE   (LEEBRAY)
Imagine giving someone his LIBERTY and
setting him FREE.

○ The Spanish for DEEP is PROFUNDO   (PROFOONDO)
Imagine thinking DEEP, PROFOUND
thoughts.

○ The Spanish for OLD is VIEJO   (VEE EHO)
Imagine saying: "Goodbye OLD man, WE
HATE YOU."

○ The Spanish for LITTLE is PEQUEÑO   (PEKENYO)
Imagine a LITTLE BIKINI.

YOU CAN WRITE YOUR ANSWERS IN

○ What is the English for viejo? _____

○ What is the English for profundo? _____

○ What is the English for libre? _____

○ What is the English for bonito? _____

○ What is the English for pequeño? _____

TURN BACK FOR THE ANSWERS

COVER UP THE LEFT HAND PAGE BEFORE ANSWERING

○ What is the Spanish for old?   _____

○ What is the Spanish for deep?   _____

○ What is the Spanish for free?   _____

○ What is the Spanish for pretty?   _____

○ What is the Spanish for little?   _____

TURN BACK FOR THE ANSWERS

ELEMENTARY GRAMMAR

You will remember from the last section that the ending of an adjective always agrees with the noun.

For example,

EL TORO ESTÁ BONITO is THE BULL IS PRETTY

LA VACA ESTÁ BONITA is THE COW IS PRETTY

You will probably have noticed, however, that you have been given some adjectives which do not end in "o" or "a", like LIBRE for FREE.

When this happens, you just leave the adjective alone, whatever it goes with.

For example:

THE BULL IS FREE is EL TORO ESTÁ LIBRE

THE COW IS FREE   is LA VACA ESTÁ LIBRE

Now cover up the answers below and translate the following:

(You can write your answers in)

1. THE QUICK JELLYFISH IS QUIET
2. THE QUIET WASP IS FREE
3. THE PRETTY CHICKEN IS FRESH
4. THE QUIET DOG IS FRESH
5. THE BLACK PIG IS FREE

The answers are:

1. LA MEDUSA RÁPIDA ESTÁ TRANQUILA
2. LA AVISPA TRANQUILA ESTÁ LIBRE
3. EL POLLO BONITO ESTÁ FRESCO
4. EL PERRO TRANQUILO ESTÁ FRESCO
5. EL PUERCO NEGRO ESTÁ LIBRE

Now cover up the answers below and translate the following:

(You can write your answers in)

1. EL BURRO NEGRO ESTÁ LIBRE
2. EL SALMÓN BONITO ESTÁ FRESCO
3. EL PATO VERDE ESTÁ LIBRE
4. LA RATA BLANCA ESTÁ RÁPIDA
5. EL TORO NEGRO ESTÁ LIBRE

The answers are:

1. THE BLACK DONKEY IS FREE
2. THE PRETTY SALMON IS FRESH
3. THE GREEN DUCK IS FREE
4. THE WHITE RAT IS QUICK
5. THE BLACK BULL IS FREE

MORE FURNITURE AND FITTINGS

THINK OF EACH IMAGE IN YOUR MIND'S EYE FOR ABOUT TEN SECONDS

○ The Spanish for STAIRS is ESCALERA   (ESKALERA)
  Imagine ESCALATORS in your house instead of stairs.

○ The Spanish for FLOOR is SUELO   (SOO ELO)
  Imagine a big SWELLING rising up in the floor.

○ The Spanish for WALL is (LA) PARED   (PARED)
  Imagine watching a PARADE from the top of a high wall.

○ The Spanish for KITCHEN is COCINA   (KOTHEENA)
  Imagine being COSY IN A kitchen.

○ The Spanish for BEDROOM is DORMITORIO
  Imagine your bedroom has been turned   (DORMEETORYO)
  into a DORMITORY, with lots of people sleeping in it.

○ The Spanish for DOOR is PUERTA   (POO ERTA)
  Imagine a hotel PORTER opening a door for you.

○ The Spanish for WINDOW is VENTANA   (VENTANA)
  Imagine a German fly that VENT ON A window.

○ The Spanish for GARDEN is JARDÍN   (HARDEEN)
  Imagine someone working HARD IN the garden.

○ The Spanish for DINING ROOM is COMEDOR (KOMEDOR)
  Imagine entertaining an Air COMMODORE
  to dinner in your dining room.

○ The Spanish for CLOAKROOM is (EL)   (GOO ARDARROPA)
  GUARDARROPA
  Imagine someone paid to GUARD A ROPE in a cloakroom.

  (N.B. This is masculine even though it ends in "a".)

YOU CAN WRITE YOUR ANSWERS IN

○ What is the English for (el) guardarropa? _____

○ What is the English for comedor? _____

○ What is the English for jardín? _____

○ What is the English for ventana? _____

○ What is the English for puerta? _____

○ What is the English for dormitorio? _____

○ What is the English for cocina? _____

○ What is the English for (la) pared? _____

○ What is the English for suelo? _____

○ What is the English for escalera? _____

TURN BACK FOR THE ANSWERS

YOU CAN WRITE YOUR ANSWERS IN

○ What is the Spanish for cloakroom? _____

○ What is the Spanish for dining room? _____

○ What is the Spanish for garden? _____

○ What is the Spanish for window? _____

○ What is the Spanish for door? _____

○ What is the Spanish for bedroom? _____

○ What is the Spanish for kitchen? _____

○ What is the Spanish for wall? _____

○ What is the Spanish for floor? _____

○ What is the Spanish for stairs? _____

TURN BACK FOR THE ANSWERS

SOME USEFUL VERBS

○ The Spanish for HAS is TIENE   (TEE ENAY)
   Imagine someone HAS a TINNY hat.

○ The Spanish for WANTS is QUIERE   (KEE ERAY)
   Imagine someone who WANTS to QUERY everything.

○ The Spanish for EATS is COME   (KOMAY)
   Imagine telling someone to COME IN and
   EAT.

YOU CAN WRITE YOUR ANSWERS IN

○ What is the English for come? _____

○ What is the English for quiere? _____

○ What is the English for tiene? _____

TURN BACK FOR THE ANSWERS

COVER UP THE LEFT HAND PAGE BEFORE ANSWERING

○ What is the Spanish for eats? _____

○ What is the Spanish for wants? _____

○ What is the Spanish for has? _____

TURN BACK FOR THE ANSWERS

Now cover up the answers below and translate the following:

(You can write your answers in)

1. THE ELEPHANT HAS THE GOAT
2. THE FROG HAS THE QUIET CAT
3. THE BLACK BEAR WANTS THE TABLE
4. THE COW EATS THE QUIET BIRD
5. THE DOG EATS THE CURTAIN

The answers are:

1. EL ELEFANTE TIENE LA CABRA
2. LA RANA TIENE EL GATO TRANQUILO
3. EL OSO NEGRO QUIERE LA MESA
4. LA VACA COME EL PÁJARO TRANQUILO
5. EL PERRO COME LA CORTINA

Now cover up the answers below and translate the following:

(You can write your answers in)

1. EL BURRO QUIERE LA CAMA VIEJA
2. EL MONO QUIERE LA CAMA PROFUNDA
3. EL OSO TIENE EL PIANO GRIS
4. LA ABEJA COME LA CORTINA BONITA
5. LA AVISPA QUIERE LA SILLA DURA

The answers are:

1. THE DONKEY WANTS THE OLD BED
2. THE MONKEY WANTS THE DEEP BED
3. THE BEAR HAS THE GREY PIANO
4. THE BEE EATS THE PRETTY CURTAIN
5. THE WASP WANTS THE HARD CHAIR

Section 3 CLOTHES/FAMILY WORDS

CLOTHES

THINK OF EACH IMAGE IN YOUR MIND'S EYE FOR ABOUT TEN SECONDS

○ The Spanish for HAT is SOMBRERO   (SOMBRERO)
Imagine being given a large SOMBRERO
when you ask for a hat.

○ The Spanish for SHOE is ZAPATO   (THAPATO)
Imagine a shoe on THE PATIO.

○ The Spanish for TROUSERS is   (PANTALONES)
PANTALONES
Imagine wearing baggy PANTALOONS for trousers.

○ The Spanish for SKIRT is FALDA   (FALDA)
Imagine you FOLD A skirt away.

○ The Spanish for BLOUSE is BLUSA   (BLOOSA)
Imagine a BLUE blouse.

○ The Spanish for COAT is ABRIGO   (ABREEGO)
Imagine someone throwing APRICOTS at your coat.

○ The Spanish for SHIRT is CAMISA   (KAMEESA)
Imagine shouting "COME HERE SIR and get your shirt."

○ The Spanish for DRESS is VESTIDO   (VESTEEDO)
Imagine telling a little girl after putting her
dress on that she should wear a VESTI TOO!

○ The Spanish for SANDAL is SANDALIA   (SANDALYA)
Imagine a bullfighter in SANDALS.

○ The Spanish for BATHING TRUNKS is   (BANYADOR)
BAÑADOR
Imagine you BANG THE DOOR with your bathing trunks.

59

YOU CAN WRITE YOUR ANSWERS IN

○ What is the English for bañador? _____

○ What is the English for sandalia? _____

○ What is the English for vestido? _____

○ What is the English for camisa? _____

○ What is the English for abrigo? _____

○ What is the English for blusa? _____

○ What is the English for falda? _____

○ What is the English for pantalones? _____

○ What is the English for zapato? _____

○ What is the English for sombrero? _____

TURN BACK FOR THE ANSWERS

COVER UP THE LEFT HAND PAGE BEFORE ANSWERING

○ What is the Spanish for bathing trunks? _____

○ What is the Spanish for sandal? _____

○ What is the Spanish for dress? _____

○ What is the Spanish for shirt? _____

○ What is the Spanish for coat? _____

○ What is the Spanish for blouse? _____

○ What is the Spanish for skirt? _____

○ What is the Spanish for trousers? _____

○ What is the Spanish for shoe? _____

○ What is the Spanish for hat? _____

TURN BACK FOR THE ANSWERS

FAMILY

THINK OF EACH IMAGE IN YOUR MIND'S EYE FOR ABOUT TEN SECONDS

○ The Spanish for FATHER is PADRE　　　　(PADRAY)
Imagine your father dressed up as a PADRE.

○ The Spanish for MOTHER is MADRE　　　　(MADRAY)
Imagine your mother very MAD at you.

○ The Spanish for BROTHER is HERMANO　　(ERMANO)
Imagine your brother dressed up as an
AIRMAN, with wings on his shoulder.

○ The Spanish for SISTER is HERMANA　　(ERMANA)
Imagine your sister also dressed as an AIRMAN.
(But the word ends in "A" not "O".)

○ The Spanish for HUSBAND is MARIDO　　(MAREEDO)
Imagine your husband is MARRIED!

○ The Spanish for WIFE is MUJER　　　　(MOOHER)
Imagine your wife is dressed in a MOHAIR coat.

○ The Spanish for BOY is MUCHACHO　　(MOOCHACHO)
Imagine a boy who MOOS when a CHAT-
SHOW comes on: MOO-CHA-CHO.

○ The Spanish for GIRL is MUCHACHA　　(MOOCHACHA)
Imagine a girl who MOOS, then does a
CHA-CHA: MOO-CHA-CHA.

○ The Spanish for SON is HIJO　　　　　　(EEHO)
Imagine your son going EE-HO, just like a donkey.

○ The Spanish for DAUGHTER is HIJA　　(EEHA)
Imagine your daughter sounding like a
female donkey, with an "a" at the end: EE-HA.

YOU CAN WRITE YOUR ANSWERS IN

○ What is the English for hija? _____

○ What is the English for hijo? _____

○ What is the English for muchacha? _____

○ What is the English for muchacho? _____

○ What is the English for mujer? _____

○ What is the English for marido? _____

○ What is the English for hermana? _____

○ What is the English for hermano? _____

○ What is the English for madre? _____

○ What is the English for padre? _____

TURN BACK FOR THE ANSWERS

COVER UP THE LEFT HAND PAGE BEFORE ANSWERING

○ What is the Spanish for daughter? _____

○ What is the Spanish for son? _____

○ What is the Spanish for girl? _____

○ What is the Spanish for boy? _____

○ What is the Spanish for wife? _____

○ What is the Spanish for husband? _____

○ What is the Spanish for sister? _____

○ What is the Spanish for brother? _____

○ What is the Spanish for mother? _____

○ What is the Spanish for father? _____

TURN BACK FOR THE ANSWERS

A FEW USEFUL WORDS

THINK OF EACH IMAGE IN YOUR MIND'S EYE FOR ABOUT TEN SECONDS

○ The Spanish for ONLY is SOLAMENTE   (SOLAMENTAY)
   Imagine thinking 'If ONLY SOLOMON MEANT IT."

○ The Spanish for VERY is MUY   (MOO EE)
   Imagine MWE are VERY good at Spanish.

○ The Spanish for YES is SÍ   (SEE)
   Imagine answering "YES. SI Señor! Yes Sir."

○ The Spanish for NO is NO   (NO)
   Imagine thinking "NO! NO! Mr. Bullfighter."

○ The Spanish for NOT is NO   (NO)
   Imagine saying "No, NOT, NO!"

YOU CAN WRITE YOUR ANSWERS IN

○ What is the English for no? _____

○ What is the English for sí? _____

○ What is the English for muy? _____

○ What is the English for solamente? _____

TURN BACK FOR THE ANSWERS

COVER UP THE LEFT HAND PAGE BEFORE ANSWERING

○ What is the Spanish for no or not? _____

○ What is the Spanish for yes? _____

○ What is the Spanish for very? _____

○ What is the Spanish for only? _____

TURN BACK FOR THE ANSWERS

ELEMENTARY GRAMMAR

In this section, you will be shown how to use the words AND, BUT and OR.

The Spanish for AND is Y (pronounced EE).

So,

PRETTY AND BAD is BONITO Y MALO.

The Spanish for BUT is PERO.

This sounds like PERRO, but the sound of the R is shorter.

So,

PRETTY BUT BAD is BONITO PERO MALO.

The Spanish for OR is O.

O is the first letter of the word OR. It is as if the Spaniards have forgotten to put the R on the word.

So,

PRETTY OR BAD is BONITO O MALO.

Now cover up the answers below and translate the following:

(You can write your answers in)

1. THE DOG HAS THE HAT AND THE SKIRT
2. THE FROG WANTS THE SKIRT AND THE DRESS
3. THE FLY HAS THE BATHING TRUNKS AND THE SHIRT
4. THE FATHER EATS THE MOTHER BUT NOT THE SON
5. THE BOY WANTS THE PRETTY GOAT

The answers are:

1. EL PERRO TIENE EL SOMBRERO Y LA FALDA
2. LA RANA QUIERE LA FALDA Y EL VESTIDO
3. LA MOSCA TIENE EL BAÑADOR Y LA CAMISA
4. EL PADRE COME EL MADRE PERO NO EL HIJO
5. EL MUCHACHO QUIERE LA CABRA BONITA

Now cover up the answers below and translate the following:

(You can write your answers in)

1. EL MARIDO QUIERE EL RELOJ VIEJO PERO NO EL PIANO

2. EL GATO PEQUEÑO QUIERE EL CAJÓN O EL ARMARIO

3. LA MUCHACHA BONITA TIENE EL ESTANTE GRIS

4. LA MOSCA AZUL COME LA PUERTA AMARILLA

5. EL HERMANO QUIERE EL GUARDARROPA Y LA HERMANA QUIERE EL DORMITORIO

The answers are:

1. THE HUSBAND WANTS THE OLD CLOCK BUT NOT THE PIANO

2. THE LITTLE CAT WANTS THE DRAWER OR THE CUPBOARD

3. THE PRETTY GIRL HAS THE GREY SHELF

4. THE BLUE FLY EATS THE YELLOW DOOR

5. THE BROTHER WANTS THE CLOAKROOM AND THE SISTER WANTS THE BEDROOM

SOME MORE ELEMENTARY GRAMMAR

The next grammar point is about the word A.

The Spanish for this word as used in A PIG or A CAT or AN ANIMAL is UN, (pronounced OON).

For example:

A PIG is UN PUERCO

A DOG is UN PERRO

A CAT is UN GATO

When the word is feminine, then you add the feminine ending A to the word UN to make UNA (pronounced OONA).

For example:

A COW   is UNA VACA

A GOAT   is UNA CABRA

A TABLE is UNA MESA

Now cover up the answers below and translate the following:

(You can write your answers in)

1. A RED COW EATS A WINDOW
2. A WIFE WANTS A DINING ROOM AND A KITCHEN
3. A BAD PIG WANTS A SHOE
4. A BEAR HAS A FRESH SHIRT AND A FRESH COAT
5. A QUICK RAT WANTS A QUIET BED

The answers are:

1. UNA VACA ROJA COME UNA VENTANA
2. UNA MUJER QUIERE UN COMEDOR Y UNA COCINA
3. UN PUERCO MALO QUIERE UN ZAPATO
4. UN OSO TIENE UNA CAMISA FRESCA Y UN ABRIGO FRESCO
5. UNA RATA RÁPIDA QUIERE UNA CAMA TRANQUILA

Now cover up the answers below and translate the following:

(You can write your answers in)

1. UN ANIMAL TIENE UN ARMARIO DURO
2. EL PUERCO QUIERE UN GUARDARROPA
3. EL PÁJARO BONITO TIENE UN JARDÍN VERDE
4. EL PATO QUIERE EL COMEDOR
5. UN POLLO TIENE UN ESTANTE VERDE

The answers are:

1. AN ANIMAL HAS A HARD CUPBOARD
2. THE PIG WANTS A CLOAKROOM
3. THE PRETTY BIRD HAS A GREEN GARDEN
4. THE DUCK WANTS THE DINING ROOM
5. A CHICKEN HAS A GREEN SHELF

A NUMBER OF USEFUL WORDS

THINK OF EACH IMAGE IN YOUR MIND'S EYE FOR ABOUT TEN SECONDS

○ The Spanish for FRIEND is AMIGO   (AMEEGO)
Imagine telling my friend that I MAY
GO if he is not more pleasant to me.

○ The Spanish for AFTERNOON is (LA) TARDE   (TARDAY)
Imagine being so late and TARDY at
getting up that it is the afternoon before your appear.

○ The Spanish for STORM is TORMENTA   (TORMENTA)
Imagine being TORMENTED by a storm.

○ The Spanish for RECEPTIONIST is   (RETHEPTHEE
RECEPCIONISTA   ONEESTA)
Imagine a bullfighter asking a
RECEPTIONIST for a room.

○ The Spanish for NUMBER is NÚMERO   (NOOMERO)
Imagine someone giving you
NUMEROUS numbers for his telephone number.

○ The Spanish for PAPER is PAPEL   (PAPEL)
Imagine everyone throwing paper during a PAPAL visit.

○ The Spanish for ROOM is (LA)   (ABEETATHYON)
HABITACIÓN
Imagine thinking "This room is not fit
for human HABITATION".

○ The Spanish for LETTER BOX is BUZÓN   (BOOTHON)
Imagine a BOOTH ON top of a letter box.

○ The Spanish for BATH is BAÑO   (BANYO)
Imagine they BAN YOU from having a bath.

○ The Spanish for MORNING is MAÑANA   (MANYANA)
Imagine meeting a MAN YOU KNOW every morning.

YOU CAN WRITE YOUR ANSWERS IN

○ What is the English for mañana? _____

○ What is the English for baño? _____

○ What is the English for buzón? _____

○ What is the English for (la) habitación? _____

○ What is the English for papel? _____

○ What is the English for número? _____

○ What is the English for recepcionista? _____

○ What is the English for tormenta? _____

○ What is the English for (la) tarde? _____

○ What is the English for amigo? _____

TURN BACK FOR THE ANSWERS

COVER UP THE LEFT HAND PAGE BEFORE ANSWERING

○ What is the Spanish for morning?   _____

○ What is the Spanish for bath?   _____

○ What is the Spanish for letter box?   _____

○ What is the Spanish for room?   _____

○ What is the Spanish for paper?   _____

○ What is the Spanish for number?   _____

○ What is the Spanish for receptionist?   _____

○ What is the Spanish for storm?   _____

○ What is the Spanish for afternoon?   _____

○ What is the Spanish for friend?   _____

TURN BACK FOR THE ANSWERS

Now cover up the answers below and translate the following:

(You can write your answers in)

1. A FRIEND EATS A RECEPTIONIST
2. A DOG WANTS A RED BATH AND A RED LETTER BOX
3. A BLACK CAT WANTS THE WHITE PAPER AND A QUIET ROOM
4. THE DOG WANTS THE BLACK PAPER AND THE CAT HAS A NUMBER
5. THE MORNING IS FRESH AND THE AFTERNOON IS FRESH

The answers are:

1. UN AMIGO COME UNA RECEPCIONISTA
2. UN PERRO QUIERE UN BAÑO ROJO Y UN BUZÓN ROJO
3. UN GATO NEGRO QUIERE EL PAPEL BLANCO Y UNA HABITACIÓN TRANQUILA
4. EL PERRO QUIERE EL PAPEL NEGRO Y EL GATO TIENE UN NÚMERO
5. LA MAÑANA ESTÁ FRESCA Y LA TARDE ESTÁ FRESCA

Now cover up the answers below and translate the following:

(You can write your answers in)

1. EL PERRO QUIERE UN BUZÓN

2. LA TORMENTA ESTÁ TRANQUILA

3. LA RECEPCIONISTA QUIERE UN NÚMERO

4. LA MAÑANA ESTÁ TRANQUILA Y LA TARDE ESTÁ TRANQUILA

5. EL AMIGO ESTÁ RÁPIDO

The answers are:

1. THE DOG WANTS A LETTER BOX

2. THE STORM IS QUIET

3. THE RECEPTIONIST WANTS A NUMBER

4. THE MORNING IS QUIET AND THE AFTERNOON IS QUIET

5. THE FRIEND IS QUICK

Section 4   IN THE COUNTRY/TIME WORDS

IN THE COUNTRY

THINK OF EACH IMAGE IN YOUR MIND'S EYE FOR ABOUT TEN SECONDS

○ The Spanish for FLOWER is (LA) FLOR   (FLOR)
  Imagine buying flowers from a FLORist.

○ The Spanish for TREE is ÁRBOL   (ARBOL)
  Imagine throwing a HARD BALL against a tree.

○ The Spanish for PLANT is PLANTA   (PLANTA)
  Imagine giving a bullfighter a potted PLANT.

○ The Spanish for FRUIT is FRUTA   (FROOTA)
  Imagine throwing FRUIT at a bullfighter.

○ The Spanish for PATH is SENDA   (SENDA)
  Imagine you SEND A friend along a path.

YOU CAN WRITE YOUR ANSWERS IN

○ What is the English for senda?   _____

○ What is the English for fruta?   _____

○ What is the English for planta?   _____

○ What is the English for árbol?   _____

○ What is the English for (la) flor?   _____

TURN BACK FOR THE ANSWERS

COVER UP THE LEFT HAND PAGE BEFORE ANSWERING

○ What is the Spanish for path? _____

○ What is the Spanish for fruit? _____

○ What is the Spanish for plant? _____

○ What is the Spanish for tree? _____

○ What is the Spanish for flower? _____

TURN BACK FOR THE ANSWERS

TIME

THINK OF EACH IMAGE IN YOUR MIND'S EYE FOR ABOUT TEN SECONDS

○ The Spanish for TIME is TIEMPO   (TEE EMPO)
Imagine keeping time to the TEMPO of the music.

○ The Spanish for SECOND is SEGUNDO   (SEGOONDO)
Imagine a bullfighter tapping his feet every SECOND.

○ The Spanish for MINUTE is MINUTO   (MEENOOTO)
Imagine a bullfighter killing a bull once a MINUTE.

○ The Spanish for HOUR is HORA   (ORA)
Imagine waiting in HORROR for the hour to strike.

○ The Spanish for WEEK is SEMANA   (SEMANA)
Imagine going to a SEMINAR once a week.

○ The Spanish for MONTH is MES   (MES)
Imagine being in a MESS once a month.

○ The Spanish for YEAR is AÑO   (ANYO)
Imagine a year is ANNUAL.

○ The Spanish for DAY is (EL) DÍA   (DEE A)
Imagine thinking everything is DEAR during the day.
(N.B. This is masculine even though it ends in "a".)

○ The Spanish for NIGHT is (LA) NOCHE   (NOCHAY)
Imagine NOCTURNAL animals are out at night.

○ The Spanish for YESTERDAY is AYER   (A YER)
Imagine thinking that prices were HIGHER yesterday.

YOU CAN WRITE YOUR ANSWERS IN

○ What is the English for ayer? _____

○ What is the English for (la) noche? _____

○ What is the English for (el) día? _____

○ What is the English for año? _____

○ What is the English for mes? _____

○ What is the English for semana? _____

○ What is the English for hora? _____

○ What is the English for minuto? _____

○ What is the English for segundo? _____

○ What is the English for tiempo? _____

TURN BACK FOR THE ANSWERS

COVER UP THE LEFT HAND PAGE BEFORE ANSWERING

○ What is the Spanish for yesterday? _____

○ What is the Spanish for night? _____

○ What is the Spanish for day? _____

○ What is the Spanish for year? _____

○ What is the Spanish for month? _____

○ What is the Spanish for week? _____

○ What is the Spanish for hour? _____

○ What is the Spanish for minute? _____

○ What is the Spanish for second? _____

○ What is the Spanish for time? _____

TURN BACK FOR THE ANSWERS

SOME MORE USEFUL WORDS

THINK OF EACH IMAGE IN YOUR MIND'S EYE FOR ABOUT TEN SECONDS

○ The Spanish for SOON is PRONTO   (PRONTO)
Imagine telling someone that they had
better do something SOON, PRONTO.

○ The Spanish for MUCH is MUCHO   (MOOCHO)
Imagine someone who MOOCHES from you
MUCH of the time.
(MUCHO and MUCH also sound similar)

○ The Spanish for MORE is MÁS   (MAS)
Imagine being given a MASS of food, and
your host giving you MORE and more.

○ The Spanish for LESS is MENOS   (MENOS)
Imagine getting LESS — a MINUS quantity.

○ The Spanish for ALWAYS is SIEMPRE   (SEE EMPRAY)
Imagine someone who ALWAYS SIMPERS.

YOU CAN WRITE YOUR ANSWERS IN

○ What is the English for siempre? _____

○ What is the English for menos? _____

○ What is the English for más? _____

○ What is the English for mucho? _____

○ What is the English for pronto? _____

TURN BACK FOR THE ANSWERS

COVER UP THE LEFT HAND PAGE BEFORE ANSWERING

○ What is the Spanish for always?   _____

○ What is the Spanish for less?   _____

○ What is the Spanish for more?   _____

○ What is the Spanish for much?   _____

○ What is the Spanish for soon?   _____

TURN BACK FOR THE ANSWERS

ELEMENTARY GRAMMAR

In the first section we learned that the Spanish for IS is ESTÁ.

For example:

LA VACA ESTÁ FRESCA is THE COW IS FRESH

There are, however, two words for the word IS in Spanish — ESTÁ and ES.

(ES is pronounced like the letter "S")

You use ESTÁ for something temporary, and ES for something permanent.

For example:

If you mean by THE DOG IS QUICK that it is a quick dog, it always moves quickly and so on, then the Spanish is:

EL PERRO ES RÁPIDO (It is a quick dog)

If, on the other hand, you mean that the dog was quick just now, when it ran away, then the Spanish is:

EL PERRO ESTÁ RÁPIDO.

Here is another example:

THE CAT IS GOOD

In Spanish EL GATO ES BUENO means it is a good cat.

EL GATO ESTÁ BUENO means that it is being good at the minute.

If you use the word TODAY this will almost always mean that the description will be temporary and you would use the word ESTÁ.

The Spanish word for TODAY is HOY.

Imagine thinking "OY! Today's the day."

So, the sentence THE CAT IS GOOD TODAY is: EL GATO ESTÁ BUENO HOY.

94

Now cover up the answers below and translate the following:

(You can write your answers in)

1. LA SANDALIA ES NEGRA
2. EL ÁRBOL ES MUY PEQUEÑO
3. EL PEZ ESTÁ FRESCO
4. LA SENDA ES VERDE Y LA PLANTA ES BLANCA
5. LA CAMA ES SOLAMENTE DURA

The answers are:

1. THE SANDAL IS BLACK
2. THE TREE IS VERY SMALL
3. THE FISH IS FRESH
4. THE PATH IS GREEN AND THE PLANT IS WHITE
5. THE BED IS ONLY HARD

Now cover up the answers below and translate the following:

(You can write your answers in)

1. THE COW IS QUICK (it is a quick cow)
2. THE MOUSE IS QUICK (the mouse moved quickly)
3. THE DONKEY IS QUIET (the donkey is quiet at the minute)
4. THE ELEPHANT IS QUIET (it is a quiet elephant)
5. THE FLY IS FRESH (the fly is fresh now)

The answers are:

1. LA VACA ES RÁPIDA
2. EL RATÓN ESTÁ RÁPIDO
3. EL BURRO ESTÁ TRANQUILO
4. EL ELEFANTE ES TRANQUILO
5. LA MOSCA ESTÁ FRESCA

You must not worry if you do not get everything right at this stage. This is about the hardest part of the grammar.

All you need to remember is why ES and ESTÁ are different.

ELEMENTARY GRAMMAR

The Spanish for ARE is SON, if ARE is meant in the permanent sense.

So,

THE DOG AND THE CAT ARE QUIET is EL PERRO Y EL GATO SON TRANQUILOS.

If ARE is used in a temporary sense, then the Spanish word for it is ESTÁN.

So,

THE DOG AND THE CAT ARE QUIET TODAY is EL PERRO Y EL GATO ESTÁN TRANQUILOS HOY

Please note that you have to make the adjective plural too, so you make TRANQUILO into TRANQUILOS.

You should also note:

When you have a masculine and feminine word together, like THE DOG AND THE FROG ARE BLACK, then the end of the adjective (NEGRO) is always MASCULINE and plural.

So,

THE DOG AND THE FROG ARE BLACK is EL PERRO Y LA RANA SON NEGROS.

Now cover up the answers below and translate the following:

(You can write your answers in)

1. THE BED AND THE TABLE ARE ALWAYS BLACK
2. THE BLUE CURTAIN AND THE GREEN DRAWER ARE OLD
3. THE GARDEN AND THE COAT ARE FRESH AND GREEN
4. THE COW AND THE BULL ARE VERY GOOD
5. THE SHIRT AND THE COAT ARE ALWAYS BLACK

The answers are:

1. LA CAMA Y LA MESA SON SIEMPRE NEGRAS
2. LA CORTINA AZUL Y EL CAJÓN VERDE SON VIEJOS
3. EL JARDÍN Y EL ABRIGO SON FRESCOS Y VERDES
4. LA VACA Y EL TORO SON (or ESTÁN) MUY BUENOS
5. LA CAMISA Y EL ABRIGO SON SIEMPRE NEGROS

Now cover up the answers below and translate the following:

(You can write your answers in)

1. EL SUELO Y LA PARED SON SOLAMENTE AMARILLOS
2. LA FLOR Y EL ÁRBOL ESTÁN MUY BONITOS HOY
3. EL BAÑO ES MUY PROFUNDO
4. LA PLANTA Y LA CAMISA SON ROJAS
5. EL OSO ESTÁ MALO

The answers are:

1. THE FLOOR AND THE WALL ARE ONLY YELLOW
2. THE FLOWER AND THE TREE ARE VERY PRETTY TODAY
3. THE BATH IS VERY DEEP
4. THE PLANT AND THE SHIRT ARE RED
5. THE BEAR IS BAD

THE DAYS OF THE WEEK

THINK OF EACH IMAGE IN YOUR MIND'S EYE FOR ABOUT TEN SECONDS

○ The Spanish for MONDAY is LUNES   (LOONAYS)
Imagine only LOONIES go to work on Monday.

○ The Spanish for TUESDAY is MARTES   (MARTAYS)
Imagine you always burn MARTYRS on Tuesdays.

○ The Spanish for WEDNESDAY is MIÉRCOLES
Imagine praying for MIRACLES on   (MEE ERCOLAYS)
Wednesday so that the end of the week will come quickly.

○ The Spanish for THURSDAY is JUEVES   (HOO EVAYS)
Imagine you WAVE US good-bye on Thursdays.

○ The Spanish for FRIDAY is VIERNES   (VEE ERNAYS)
Imagine showing your BARE KNEES
on Friday, to celebrate the end of the week.

○ The Spanish for SATURDAY is SÁBADO   (SABADO)
Imagine Saturday is the Jewish SABBATH.

○ The Spanish for SUNDAY is DOMINGO   (DOMEENGO)
Imagine you play DOMINOES with your
family on Sunday evening before pushing them off to bed.

YOU CAN WRITE YOUR ANSWERS IN

○ What is the English for domingo? _____

○ What is the English for sábado? _____

○ What is the English for viernes? _____

○ What is the English for jueves? _____

○ What is the English for miércoles? _____

○ What is the English for martes? _____

○ What is the English for lunes? _____

TURN BACK FOR THE ANSWERS

COVER UP THE LEFT HAND PAGE BEFORE ANSWERING

○ What is the Spanish for Sunday? _____

○ What is the Spanish for Saturday? _____

○ What is the Spanish for Friday? _____

○ What is the Spanish for Thursday? _____

○ What is the Spanish for Wednesday? _____

○ What is the Spanish for Tuesday? _____

○ What is the Spanish for Monday? _____

TURN BACK FOR THE ANSWERS

PLEASE NOTE:
You do not say the word ON when talking about the days of the week; you miss the word ON out and use EL.

So, ON TUESDAY is EL MARTES, if you mean NEXT TUESDAY.

If you mean EVERY TUESDAY (as you would if you said ON TUESDAYS) then in Spanish you make it plural and use LOS.

So,

ON TUESDAYS is LOS MARTES

ON SUNDAYS   is LOS DOMINGOS

and so on.

THE DOG EATS ON TUESDAYS   is EL PERRO COME
LOS MARTES.

THE COW EATS ON SATURDAYS is LA VACA COME
LOS SÁBADOS.

Now cover up the answers below and translate the following:

(You can write your answers in)

1. LOS MARTES EL PERRO COME LA FRUTA
2. EL PERRO COME LOS LUNES, LOS VIERNES, LOS SÁBADOS Y LOS DOMINGOS
3. NO, EL GATO NO COME LOS JUEVES Y LOS MIÉRCOLES
4. LOS DOMINGOS LA NOCHE ESTÁ PRONTO NEGRA
5. EL BURRO QUIERE MENOS PATO Y MÁS POLLO

The answers are:

1. ON TUESDAYS THE DOG EATS THE FRUIT
2. THE DOG EATS ON MONDAYS, FRIDAYS, SATURDAYS AND SUNDAYS
3. NO, THE CAT DOES NOT EAT ON THURSDAYS AND WEDNESDAYS
4. ON SUNDAYS THE NIGHT IS SOON BLACK
5. THE DONKEY WANTS LESS DUCK AND MORE CHICKEN

ELEMENTARY GRAMMAR

The way to ask questions in Spanish when you are speaking is by tone of voice; you do not need to change the word order.

¿ES UN TORO? is IS IT A BULL?

In Spanish you miss out words like HE, I, YOU, IT, and so on.

So,

IT IS A BULL	is ES UN TORO
HE HAS A BULL	is TIENE UN TORO
HAS HE A BULL?	is also ¿TIENE UN TORO?
DOES HE HAVE A BULL?	is also ¿TIENE UN TORO?

Note the use of the upside-down question mark in written Spanish, which indicates that a question is coming up.

Now cover up the answers below and translate the following:

(You can write your answers in)

1. IS IT A PIG?
2. HE HAS A DOG
3. IS IT A TABLE?
4. HAS HE A FLOWER? or DOES HE HAVE A FLOWER?
5. HE EATS A GOAT

The answers are:

1. ¿ES UN PUERCO?
2. TIENE UN PERRO?
3. ¿ES UNA MESA?
4. ¿TIENE UNA FLOR?
5. COME UNA CABRA?

Now cover up the answers below and translate the following:

(You can write your answers in)

1. ES LA SEMANA, LA HORA Y EL DÍA
2. ¿ES UN ÁRBOL VERDE?
3. ¿ES LA NOCHE?
4. ¿ES LA SENDA O LA ESCALERA?
5. ES LA HIJA, NO EL HIJO

The answers are:

1. IT IS THE WEEK, THE HOUR AND THE DAY
2. IS IT A GREEN TREE?
3. IS IT THE NIGHT?
4. IS IT THE PATH OR THE STAIRS?
5. IT IS THE DAUGHTER, NOT THE SON

Section 5 IN THE RESTAURANT, NUMBERS, TELLING THE TIME

IN THE RESTAURANT

THINK OF EACH IMAGE IN YOUR MIND'S EYE FOR ABOUT TEN SECONDS

○ The Spanish for RESTAURANT is   (RESTA
RESTAURANTE   OORANTAY)
Imagine a bullfighter in your RESTAURANT.

○ The Spanish for WAITRESS is   (KAMARERA)
CAMARERA
Imagine a waitress with a CAMERA slung around her neck.

○ The Spanish for CUP is TAZA   (TATHA)
Imagine a cup with a TASSLE dangling from the handle.

○ The Spanish for BILL is CUENTA   (KOO ENTA)
Imagine your friend WENT Away when it
came to paying the bill.

○ The Spanish for MENU is MENÚ   (MENOO)
Imagine a bullfighter studying the MENU.

○ The Spanish for PLATE is PLATO   (PLATO)
Imagine you climb a mountain and reach a
PLATEAU all covered with white plates.

○ The Spanish for KNIFE is CUCHILLO   (KOOCHEELYO)
Imagine someone with a knife saying
"With this I COULD CHILL YOU".

○ The Spanish for FORK is TENEDOR   (TENEDOR)
Imagine prodding a piece of meat with a
fork to make sure it is TENDER.

○ The Spanish for TABLECLOTH is MANTEL   (MANTEL)
Imagine a tablecloth on the MANTLEpiece.

○ The Spanish for BOTTLE is BOTELLA   (BOTELYA)
Imagine throwing a BOTTLE at a bullfighter.

YOU CAN WRITE YOUR ANSWERS IN

○ What is the English for botella? _____

○ What is the English for mantel? _____

○ What is the English for tenedor? _____

○ What is the English for cuchillo? _____

○ What is the English for plato? _____

○ What is the English for menú? _____

○ What is the English for cuenta? _____

○ What is the English for taza? _____

○ What is the English for camarera? _____

○ What is the English for restaurante? _____

TURN BACK FOR THE ANSWERS

COVER UP THE LEFT HAND PAGE BEFORE ANSWERING

○ What is the Spanish for bottle? _____

○ What is the Spanish for tablecloth? _____

○ What is the Spanish for fork? _____

○ What is the Spanish for knife? _____

○ What is the Spanish for plate? _____

○ What is the Spanish for menu? _____

○ What is the Spanish for bill? _____

○ What is the Spanish for cup? _____

○ What is the Spanish for waitress? _____

○ What is the Spanish for restaurant? _____

TURN BACK FOR THE ANSWERS

NUMBERS

THINK OF EACH IMAGE IN YOUR MIND'S EYE FOR ABOUT TEN SECONDS

○ The Spanish for ONE is UNO   (OONO)
Imagine YOU KNOW ONE.

○ The Spanish for TWO is DOS   (DOS)
Imagine you TOSS TWO coins in the air.

○ The Spanish for THREE is TRES   (TRES)
Imagine THREE TREES in front of you.

○ The Spanish for FOUR is CUATRO   (KOO ATRO)
Imagine drinking FOUR bottles of COINTREAU.

○ The Spanish for FIVE is CINCO   (THEENKO)
Imagine being bathed in the SINK O when you
were FIVE years old.

○ The Spanish for SIX is SEIS   (SE EES)
Imagine someone who SAYS SIX.

○ The Spanish for SEVEN is SIETE   (SEE ETAY)
Imagine your SETTEE has seen SEVEN deadly sins.

○ The Spanish for EIGHT is OCHO   (OCHO)
Imagine the number EIGHT painted in OCHRE.

○ The Spanish for NINE is NUEVE   (NOO EVAY)
Imagine dialling 999 for the NAVY.

○ The Spanish for ZERO is CERO   (THERO)
Imagine ZERO is NOTHING to a bullfighter.

YOU CAN WRITE YOUR ANSWERS IN

○ What is the English for uno? _____

○ What is the English for dos? _____

○ What is the English for tres? _____

○ What is the English for cuatro? _____

○ What is the English for cinco? _____

○ What is the English for seis? _____

○ What is the English for siete? _____

○ What is the English for ocho? _____

○ What is the English for nueve? _____

○ What is the English for cero? _____

TURN BACK FOR THE ANSWERS

YOU CAN WRITE YOUR ANSWERS IN

○ What is the Spanish for one? _____

○ What is the Spanish for two? _____

○ What is the Spanish for three? _____

○ What is the Spanish for four? _____

○ What is the Spanish for five? _____

○ What is the Spanish for six? _____

○ What is the Spanish for seven? _____

○ What is the Spanish for eight? _____

○ What is the Spanish for nine? _____

○ What is the Spanish for zero? _____

TURN BACK FOR THE ANSWERS

ELEMENTARY GRAMMAR: Plurals

The plurals in Spanish are very simple.

For MASCULINE plurals EL becomes LOS and the noun adds an S.

For example,

  EL PLATO   becomes LOS PLATOS (the plates)

  EL CUCHILLO   becomes LOS CUCHILLOS

  EL SOMBRERO becomes LOS SOMBREROS

For FEMININE words, the LA becomes LAS and the noun also adds an S.

For example,

  LA CABRA becomes LAS CABRAS (the goats)

  LA MESA   becomes LAS MESAS

  LA BLUSA becomes LAS BLUSAS

If a word does not end in a vowel then you simply add ES.

For example,

  EL TENEDOR becomes LOS TENEDORES (the forks)

  EL MANTEL   becomes LOS MANTELES

As we have already seen with TRANQUILOS, adjectives also add an S when they are plural.

So,

  THE FREE PIGS   is LOS PUERCOS LIBRES

  THE QUIET MICE is LOS RATONES TRANQUILOS

  THE RED TABLES is LAS MESAS ROJAS

NUMBERS DO NOT TAKE A PLURAL ENDING.

Now cover up the answers below and translate the following:

(You can write your answers in)

1. THREE CUPS ARE OLD
2. FIVE PLATES ARE VERY GOOD
3. THE KNIVES AND THE FORKS ARE VERY HARD
4. THE TABLECLOTHS AND THE BOTTLES ARE ALWAYS GREEN
5. TWO MENUS ARE VERY BAD

The answers are:

1. TRES TAZAS SON VIEJAS
2. CINCO PLATOS SON MUY BUENOS
3. LOS CUCHILLOS Y LOS TENEDORES SON MUY DUROS
4. LOS MANTELES Y LAS BOTELLAS SON SIEMPRE VERDES
5. DOS MENÚS SON MUY MALOS

Now cover up the answers below and translate the following:

(You can write your answers in)

1. SIETE DÍAS SON UNA SEMANA
2. LOS RESTAURANTES SON SIEMPRE BUENOS
3. LAS CUENTAS SON MUY BUENAS
4. LOS DÍAS SON BUENOS, Y LAS NOCHES SON BUENAS
5. LOS PANTALONES SON MUY NEGROS

The answers are:

1. SEVEN DAYS ARE A WEEK
2. THE RESTAURANTS ARE ALWAYS GOOD
3. THE BILLS ARE VERY GOOD
4. THE DAYS ARE GOOD AND THE NIGHTS ARE GOOD
5. THE TROUSERS ARE VERY BLACK

SOME MORE USEFUL WORDS

THINK OF EACH IMAGE IN YOUR MIND'S EYE FOR ABOUT TEN SECONDS

○ The Spanish for ON is EN   (EN)
  Imagine a big letter N written ON a table.

○ The Spanish for IN is also EN   (EN)
  Imagine looking IN a box and seeing a large letter N.

○ The Spanish for UNDER is DEBAJO DE   (DEBAHO DAY)
  Imagine seeing a DEBACLE UNDER DE table.

○ The Spanish for OUTSIDE is FUERA DE   (FOO ERA DAY)
  Imagine the famous discoverer of electrical
  phenomena, Michael FARADAY, OUTSIDE your house.

YOU CAN WRITE YOUR ANSWERS IN

○ What is the English for en? _____

○ What is the English for debajo de? _____

○ What is the English for fuera de? _____

TURN BACK FOR THE ANSWERS

COVER UP THE LEFT HAND PAGE BEFORE ANSWERING

○ What is the Spanish for in?   _____

○ What is the Spanish for on?   _____

○ What is the Spanish for under?   _____

○ What is the Spanish for outside?   _____

TURN BACK FOR THE ANSWERS

Please note that place words (prepositions) in Spanish are tricky and you will sometimes make mistakes. Do not worry though, as you will be understood.

There is one important point to remember:

When you use place words like IN, ON, UNDER, etc., then the word for IS is always ESTÁ, even if the thing is always in a particular place.

Now cover up the answers below and translate the following:

(You can write your answers in)

1. THE CUP IS ON THE TABLE
2. THE PLATE IS IN THE CUPBOARD
3. THE KNIFE IS UNDER A TABLE
4. THE FRUIT IS ON THE PLATE
5. A WAITRESS IS OUTSIDE A RESTAURANT

The answers are:

1. LA TAZA ESTÁ EN LA MESA
2. EL PLATO ESTÁ EN EL ARMARIO
3. EL CUCHILLO ESTÁ DEBAJO DE UNA MESA
4. LA FRUTA ESTÁ EN EL PLATO
5. UNA CAMARERA ESTÁ FUERA DE UN RESTAURANTE

Now cover up the answers below and translate the following:

(You can write your answers in)

1. SEIS CAMARERAS ESTÁN DEBAJO DE LA MESA
2. CUATRO TENEDORES ESTÁN EN EL CAJÓN
3. EL MARIDO Y LA MUJER ESTÁN EN UN RESTAURANTE
4. EL PEZ ESTÁ FUERA DE UN GUARDARROPA
5. EL PERRO ESTÁ EN EL ARMARIO AMARILLO

The answers are:

1. SIX WAITRESSES ARE UNDER THE TABLE
2. FOUR FORKS ARE IN THE DRAWER
3. THE HUSBAND AND THE WIFE ARE IN A RESTAURANT
4. THE FISH IS OUTSIDE A CLOAKROOM
5. THE DOG IS ON (or IN) THE YELLOW CUPBOARD

NUMBERS

THINK OF EACH IMAGE IN YOUR MIND'S EYE FOR ABOUT TEN SECONDS

○ The Spanish for TEN is DIEZ   (DEE ETH)
  Imagine putting someone to DEATH at ten o'clock.

○ The Spanish for ELEVEN is ONCE   (ONTHAY)
  Imagine ELEVEN footballers ON THE field.

○ The Spanish for TWELVE is DOCE   (DOTHAY)
  Imagine a DOZEN DOZY people.

○ The Spanish for TWENTY is VEINTE   (VE EENTAY)
  Imagine a German saying "Your
  vision is TVENTY-TVENTY."

○ The Spanish for TWENTY-FIVE   (VE EENTEETHEENKO)
  is VEINTICINCO
  Imagine at the age of 25 you INVENTED SINKS.

○ The Spanish for QUARTER is CUARTO   (KOO ARTO)
  Imagine asking a bullfighter for a
  QUARTER of beef.

○ The Spanish for HALF is MEDIA   (MEDYA)
  Imagine thinking it is MESSIER
  to cut someone in half than to leave them alone.

YOU CAN WRITE YOUR ANSWERS IN

○ What is the English for diez?   _____

○ What is the English for once?   _____

○ What is the English for doce?   _____

○ What is the English for veinte?   _____

○ What is the English for veinte cinco?   _____

○ What is the English for cuarto?   _____

○ What is the English for media?   _____

TURN BACK FOR THE ANSWERS

COVER UP THE LEFT HAND PAGE BEFORE ANSWERING

○ What is the Spanish for ten? _____

○ What is the Spanish for eleven? _____

○ What is the Spanish for twelve? _____

○ What is the Spanish for twenty? _____

○ What is the Spanish for twenty-five? _____

○ What is the Spanish for quarter? _____

○ What is the Spanish for half? _____

TURN BACK FOR THE ANSWERS

TELLING THE TIME

As you learned earlier, the Spanish for THE HOUR is LA HORA which is, of course, FEMININE.

The Spanish for WHAT is QUÉ (pronounced KAY) so:

WHAT TIME IS IT? is ¿QUÉ HORA ES? —

literally, WHAT HOUR IS?

To answer this question by saying, for example, IT IS ONE O'CLOCK, you say something in Spanish which translates literally as (IT) IS THE ONE: ES LA UNA.

The word HOUR is not said, but is understood.

Note that the word THE is feminine because the word HOUR is feminine.

IT IS TWO O'CLOCK becomes (THEY) ARE THE TWO or SON LAS DOS.

Here LAS is used because HORAS is plural.

Similarly,

IT IS THREE O'CLOCK   is SON LAS TRES

IT IS ELEVEN O'CLOCK is SON LAS ONCE

Now cover up the answers below and translate the following:

(You can write your answers in)

1. IT IS FIVE O'CLOCK
2. IT IS SEVEN O'CLOCK
3. IT IS NINE O'CLOCK
4. IT IS TEN O'CLOCK
5. IT IS TWO O'CLOCK

The answers are:

1. SON LAS CINCO
2. SON LAS SIETE
3. SON LAS NUEVE
4. SON LAS DIEZ
5. SON LAS DOS

TELLING THE TIME: PARTS OF AN HOUR
When you want to say IT IS QUARTER PAST or HALF PAST or FIVE PAST or TEN PAST the hour you say, for example,

THEY ARE SEVEN AND HALF or
SON LAS SIETE Y MEDIA

To say IT IS FIVE PAST THREE you say
SON LAS TRES Y CINCO

To say IT IS TWENTY PAST EIGHT you say
SON LAS OCHO Y VEINTE

When you want to say IT IS QUARTER TO THE HOUR or TWENTY TO THE HOUR or FIVE TO THE HOUR or TWENTY TO EIGHT etc., then in Spanish you say:

THEY ARE EIGHT MINUS TWENTY i.e.
SON LAS OCHO MENOS VEINTE

IT IS QUARTER TO FIVE is
SON LAS CINCO MENOS CUARTO

IT IS FIVE TO TWO is
SON LAS DOS MENOS CINCO

The only exception to this is with the hour ONE, which is singular.

So,

   IT IS QUARTER TO ONE is ES LA UNA MENOS CUARTO

Now cover up the answers below and translate the following:

(You can write your answers in)

1. IT IS HALF PAST THREE
2. IT IS FOUR O'CLOCK
3. IT IS QUARTER TO SIX
4. IT IS TEN TO SEVEN
5. IT IS HALF PAST NINE
6. IT IS TEN TO ONE
7. IT IS THREE O'CLOCK

The answers are:

1. SON LAS TRES Y MEDIA
2. SON LAS CUATRO
3. SON LAS SEIS MENOS CUARTO
4. SON LAS SIETE MENOS DIEZ
5. SON LAS NUEVE Y MEDIA
6. ES LA UNA MENOS DIEZ
7. SON LAS TRES

Section 6 FOOD AND DRINK

THINK OF EACH IMAGE IN YOUR MIND'S EYE FOR ABOUT TEN SECONDS

○ The Spanish for SOUP is SOPA   (SOPA)
Imagine a soup which tastes like SOAP.

○ The Spanish for RICE is ARROZ   (ARROTH)
Imagine someone shooting ARROWS which
land in your plate of rice.

○ The Spanish for ONION is CEBOLLA   (THEBOLYA)
Imagine one onion turning to another and
saying "THEY BOIL YOU in this place."

○ The Spanish for MUSHROOM is SETA   (SETA)
Imagine being told to SAY TA by your
mother, when she gives you a mushroom.

○ The Spanish for TOMATO is TOMATE   (TOMATAY)
Imagine throwing TOMATOES at a bullfighter.

○ The Spanish for CHEESE is QUESO   (KESO)
Imagine a CASE O' cheese.

○ The Spanish for EGG is HUEVO   (HOO EVO)
Imagine you give a WAVE O to someone who
throws eggs at you.

○ The Spanish for WATER is (EL) AGUA   (AGOO A)
Imagine an AQUADUCT bringing water to your hotel.

○ The Spanish for SUGAR is AZÚCAR   (ATHOOKAR)
Imagine stuffing A CIGAR into the sugar bowl.

○ The Spanish for COFFEE is CAFÉ   (KAFAY)
Imagine drinking coffee in a CAFE.

PLEASE NOTE: AGUA is a "funny" word; it is EL AGUA. It is a
feminine word which takes EL for THE.

YOU CAN WRITE YOUR ANSWERS IN

○ What is the English for café? _____

○ What is the English for azúcar? _____

○ What is the English for (el) agua? _____

○ What is the English for huevo? _____

○ What is the English for queso? _____

○ What is the English for tomate? _____

○ What is the English for seta? _____

○ What is the English for cebolla? _____

○ What is the English for arroz? _____

○ What is the English for sopa? _____

TURN BACK FOR THE ANSWERS

COVER UP THE LEFT HAND PAGE BEFORE ANSWERING

○ What is the Spanish for coffee? _____

○ What is the Spanish for sugar? _____

○ What is the Spanish for water? _____

○ What is the Spanish for egg? _____

○ What is the Spanish for cheese? _____

○ What is the Spanish for tomato? _____

○ What is the Spanish for mushroom? _____

○ What is the Spanish for, onion? _____

○ What is the Spanish for rice? _____

○ What is the Spanish for soup? _____

TURN BACK FOR THE ANSWERS

MORE FOOD AND DRINK WORDS

THINK OF EACH IMAGE IN YOUR MIND'S EYE FOR ABOUT TEN SECONDS

○ The Spanish for BREAD is PAN   (PAN)
  Imagine loaves of bread stuffed in a PAN.

○ The Spanish for MEAT is (LA) CARNE   (KARNAY)
  Imagine CARNIVORES eating meat.

○ The Spanish for CAULIFLOWER is
  (LA) COLIFLOR   (KOLEEFLOR)
  Imagine throwing a CAULIFLOWER at a bullfighter.

○ The Spanish for POTATO is PATATA   (PATATA)
  Imagine throwing POTATOES at a bullfighter.

○ The Spanish for WINE is VINO   (VEENO)
  Imagine a German saying "VE KNOW
  what a good wine it is."

○ The Spanish for MILK is (LA) LECHE   (LECHAY)
  Imagine LEECHES in the milk.

○ The Spanish for BEER is CERVEZA   (THERVETHA)
  Imagine demanding SERVICE for your beer in a pub.

○ The Spanish for PEAR is PERA   (PERA)
  Imagine buying a PAIR A pears.

○ The Spanish for CAKE is PASTEL   (PASTEL)
  Imagine a PASTEL coloured cake.

○ The Spanish for CABBAGE is (LA) COL   (KOL)
  Imagine you CALL someone a cabbage.

YOU CAN WRITE YOUR ANSWERS IN

○ What is the English for (la) col? _____

○ What is the English for pastel? _____

○ What is the English for pera? _____

○ What is the English for cerveza? _____

○ What is the English for (la) leche? _____

○ What is the English for vino? _____

○ What is the English for patata? _____

○ What is the English for (la) coliflor? _____

○ What is the English for (la) carne? _____

○ What is the English for pan? _____

TURN BACK FOR THE ANSWERS

COVER UP THE LEFT HAND PAGE BEFORE ANSWERING

○ What is the Spanish for cabbage? _____

○ What is the Spanish for cake? _____

○ What is the Spanish for pear? _____

○ What is the Spanish for beer? _____

○ What is the Spanish for milk? _____

○ What is the Spanish for wine? _____

○ What is the Spanish for potato? _____

○ What is the Spanish for cauliflower? _____

○ What is the Spanish for meat? _____

○ What is the Spanish for bread? _____

TURN BACK FOR THE ANSWERS

SOME MORE USEFUL WORDS

THINK OF EACH IMAGE IN YOUR MIND'S EYE FOR ABOUT TEN SECONDS

○ The Spanish for HIGH is ALTO   (ALTO)
  Imagine flying at a HIGH ALTITUDE.

○ The Spanish for LONG is LARGO   (LARGO)
  Imagine a LONG drink of LAGER.

○ The Spanish for EXPENSIVE is CARO   (KARO)
  Imagine buying an EXPENSIVE CAR.

○ The Spanish for CHEAP is BARATO   (BARATO)
  Imagine a Spanish BARITONE going
  CHEAP at auction.

○ The Spanish for DIRTY is SUCIO   (SOOTHYO)
  Imagine you SOOTHE a child who is very DIRTY.

○ The Spanish for RIGHT is CORRECTO   (KORREKTO)
  Imagine something is CORRECT and RIGHT.

○ The Spanish for WRONG is   (EENKORREKTO)
  INCORRECTO
  Imagine something is WRONG and INCORRECT.

○ The Spanish for EASY is FÁCIL   (FATHEEL)
  Imagine someone has a FACILITY for
  making things look EASY.

○ The Spanish for ANGRY is ENOJADO   (ENOHADO)
  Imagine someone being ANGRY and
  ANNOYED with us.

YOU CAN WRITE YOUR ANSWERS IN

○ What is the English for fácil? _____

○ What is the English for incorrecto? _____

○ What is the English for correcto? _____

○ What is the English for sucio? _____

○ What is the English for barato? _____

○ What is the English for caro? _____

○ What is the English for largo? _____

○ What is the English for alto? _____

○ What is the English for enojado? _____

TURN BACK FOR THE ANSWERS

COVER UP THE LEFT HAND PAGE BEFORE ANSWERING

○ What is the Spanish for easy? _____

○ What is the Spanish for wrong? _____

○ What is the Spanish for right? _____

○ What is the Spanish for dirty? _____

○ What is the Spanish for cheap? _____

○ What is the Spanish for expensive? _____

○ What is the Spanish for long? _____

○ What is the Spanish for high? _____

○ What is the Spanish for angry? _____

TURN BACK FOR THE ANSWERS

ELEMENTARY GRAMMAR

The Spanish for WAS is ESTABA when you use phrases like the following:

THE PIG WAS QUICK — EL PUERCO ESTABA RÁPIDO

THE DOG WAS DIRTY — EL PERRO ESTABA SUCIO

THE COW WAS QUIET — LA VACA ESTABA
TRANQUILA

The Spanish for WERE is ESTABAN when you use phrases like the following:

THE PIGS WERE QUICK — LOS PUERCOS ESTABAN
RÁPIDOS

THE BULLS WERE CHEAP — LOS TOROS ESTABAN
BARATOS

THE FROGS WERE DIRTY — LAS RANAS ESTABAN
SUCIAS

Now cover up the answers below and translate the following:

(You can write your answers in)

1. THE RED ONIONS WERE VERY DIRTY
2. THE PIGS AND THE DUCKS WERE ANGRY
3. THE TOMATOES WERE PRETTY
4. THE PEARS WERE CHEAP
5. THE CAULIFLOWER AND THE CABBAGE WERE DIRTY

The answers are:

1. LAS CEBOLLAS ROJAS ESTABAN MUY SUCIAS
2. LOS PUERCOS Y LOS PATOS ESTABAN ENOJADOS
3. LOS TOMATES ESTABAN BONITOS
4. LAS PERAS ESTABAN BARATAS
5. LA COLIFLOR Y LA COL ESTABAN SUCIAS

Now cover up the answers below and translate the following:

(You can write your answers in)

1. EL ARROZ ESTABA SUCIO
2. EL MENÚ ESTABA CORRECTO
3. LOS QUESOS ESTABAN FRESCOS
4. EL MENÚ ESTABA INCORRECTO
5. LAS SETAS ESTABAN ALTAS

The answers are:

1. THE RICE WAS DIRTY
2. THE MENU WAS RIGHT
3. THE CHEESES WERE FRESH
4. THE MENU WAS WRONG
5. THE MUSHROOMS WERE HIGH

SOME MORE USEFUL WORDS

THINK OF EACH IMAGE IN YOUR MIND'S EYE FOR ABOUT TEN SECONDS

○ The Spanish for FIRST is PRIMERO   (PREEMERO)
Imagine being in the FIRST, the PRIME position.

○ The Spanish for LAST is ÚLTIMO   (OOLTEEMO)
Imagine getting an ULTIMATUM for the LAST time.

○ The Spanish for HERE is AQUÍ   (AKEE)
Imagine leaving A KEY HERE.

○ The Spanish for THERE is ALLÁ   (ALYA)
Imagine shouting "Are you THERE — ALL O' YA?"

○ The Spanish for SECOND is SEGUNDO   (SEGOONDO)
Imagine a bullfighter being the SECOND
person into the ring.

NOTE:

PRIMERO and ÚLTIMO usually come before the noun as in English.

For example, THE FIRST COW is LA PRIMERA VACA

YOU CAN WRITE YOUR ANSWERS IN

○ What is the English for segundo?   _____

○ What is the English for allá?   _____

○ What is the English for aquí?   _____

○ What is the English for último?   _____

○ What is the English for primero?   _____

TURN BACK FOR THE ANSWERS

COVER UP THE LEFT HAND PAGE BEFORE ANSWERING

○ What is the Spanish for second? _____

○ What is the Spanish for there? _____

○ What is the Spanish for here? _____

○ What is the Spanish for last? _____

○ What is the Spanish for first? _____

TURN BACK FOR THE ANSWERS

Now cover up the answers below and translate the following:

(You can write your answers in)

1. THE SOUP AND THE MILK WERE HERE
2. THE WATER WAS HERE BUT THE BEER WAS THERE
3. THE LAST EGG IS HERE
4. THE COFFEE AND THE CAKE WERE HERE
5. THE MEAT IS HERE AND THE BREAD IS THERE

The answers are:

1. LA SOPA Y LA LECHE ESTABAN AQUÍ
2. EL AGUA ESTABA AQUÍ PERO LA CERVEZA ESTABA ALLÁ
3. EL ÚLTIMO HUEVO ESTÁ AQUÍ
4. EL CAFÉ Y EL PASTEL ESTABAN AQUÍ
5. LA CARNE ESTÁ AQUÍ Y EL PAN ESTÁ ALLÁ

Now cover up the answers below and translate the following:

(You can write your answers in)

1. ES LA PRIMERA VACA
2. ESTÁ AQUÍ
3. ESTÁ ALLÁ
4. ES EL ÚLTIMO TOMATE
5. ES LA SEGUNDA CEBOLLA

The answers are:

1. IT IS THE FIRST COW
2. SHE IS HERE (or HE, IT)
3. HE IS THERE (or SHE, IT)
4. IT IS THE LAST TOMATO
5. IT IS THE SECOND ONION

Section 7 SHOPPING AND BUSINESS WORDS

THINK OF EACH IMAGE IN YOUR MIND'S EYE FOR ABOUT TEN SECONDS

○ The Spanish for OWNER is   (PROPEE ETARYO)
PROPIETARIO
Imagine asking to see the
PROPRIETOR, the owner of a business.

○ The Spanish for MANAGER is DIRECTOR   (DEEREKTOR)
Imagine asking to see the manager, and
the Managing DIRECTOR being brought to see you.

○ The Spanish for BOSS is JEFE   (HEFAY)
Imagine your boss behaves like an Indian CHIEF.

○ The Spanish for JOB is EMPLEO   (EMPLEO)
Imagine being EMPLOYED to do a job.

○ The Spanish for FACTORY is FÁBRICA   (FABREEKA)
Imagine a factory making FABRICS.

○ The Spanish for SALARY is SALARIO   (SALARYO)
Imagine a bullfighter collecting a SALARY.

○ The Spanish for PRODUCT is PRODUCTO   (PRODOOKTO)
Imagine selling a bullfighter your
factory's PRODUCT.

○ The Spanish for BUSINESS is NEGOCIO   (NEGOTHYO)
Imagine having to NEGOTIATE for
your business to be successful.

○ The Spanish for CHEQUE is CHEQUE   (CHEKAY)
Imagine a bullfighter waving a CHEQUE around.

○ The Spanish for OFFICE is OFICINA   (OFEETHEENA)
Imagine a bullfighter sitting in a big
OFFICE, behind the desk.

YOU CAN WRITE YOUR ANSWERS IN

○ What is the English for oficina? _____

○ What is the English for cheque? _____

○ What is the English for negocio? _____

○ What is the English for producto? _____

○ What is the English for salario? _____

○ What is the English for fábrica? _____

○ What is the English for empleo? _____

○ What is the English for jefe? _____

○ What is the English for director? _____

○ What is the English for propietario _____

TURN BACK FOR THE ANSWERS

154

COVER THE LEFT HAND PAGE BEFORE ANSWERING

○ What is the Spanish for office? _____

○ What is the Spanish for cheque? _____

○ What is the Spanish for business? _____

○ What is the Spanish for product? _____

○ What is the Spanish for salary? _____

○ What is the Spanish for factory? _____

○ What is the Spanish for job? _____

○ What is the Spanish for boss? _____

○ What is the Spanish for manager? _____

○ What is the Spanish for owner? _____

TURN BACK FOR THE ANSWERS

MORE BUSINESS WORDS

THINK OF EACH IMAGE IN YOUR MIND'S EYE FOR ABOUT TEN SECONDS

- The Spanish for RECEIPT is RECIBO   (RETHEEBO)
  Imagine getting a RECEIPT from a bullfighter.

- The Spanish for THING is COSA   (KOSA)
  Imagine asking if that thing COST A lot.

- The Spanish for HOLIDAYS is   (VAKATHYONAYS)
  (LAS) VACACIONES
  Imagine the person you are trying to
  get hold of has gone on VACATION for his holidays.

- The Spanish for PRICE is PRECIO   (PRETHYO)
  Imagine asking an Arab street seller
  "PRAY THEE what is the price of this?"

- The Spanish for MISTAKE is ERROR   (ERROR)
  Imagine a bullfighter making a bad ERROR.

- The Spanish for MARKET is MERCADO   (MERKADO)
  Imagine a bullfighter buying goods in a MARKET.

- The Spanish for SHOP is TIENDA   (TEE ENDA)
  Imagine feeling TENDER as you enter a
  shop to buy your loved one something.

- The Spanish for SALESMAN is VENDEDOR   (VENDEDOR)
  Imagine a salesman who BENDS A DOOR
  in order to get into a business.

- The Spanish for ACCOUNTANT is CONTADOR
  Imagine an accountant sitting in his   (KONTADOR)
  office, COUNTING DOORS instead of money.

- The Spanish for MONEY is DINERO   (DEENERO)
  Imagine using your money to buy your last DINNER.

YOU CAN WRITE YOUR ANSWERS IN

○ What is the English for dinero? _____

○ What is the English for contador? _____

○ What is the English for vendedor? _____

○ What is the English for tienda? _____

○ What is the English for mercado? _____

○ What is the English for error? _____

○ What is the English for precio? _____

○ What is the English for (las) vacaciones? _____

○ What is the English for cosa? _____

○ What is the English for recibo? _____

TURN BACK FOR THE ANSWERS

COVER UP THE LEFT HAND PAGE BEFORE ANSWERING

○ What is the Spanish for money? _____

○ What is the Spanish for accountant? _____

○ What is the Spanish for salesman? _____

○ What is the Spanish for shop? _____

○ What is the Spanish for market? _____

○ What is the Spanish for mistake? _____

○ What is the Spanish for price? _____

○ What is the Spanish for holidays? _____

○ What is the Spanish for thing? _____

○ What is the Spanish for receipt? _____

YOU CAN WRITE THE ANSWERS IN

SOME MORE USEFUL WORDS

THINK OF EACH IMAGE IN YOUR MIND'S EYE FOR ABOUT TEN SECONDS

○ The Spanish for WHERE is DÓNDE   (DONDAY)
Imagine asking "WHERE on earth is DUNDEE?"

○ The Spanish for WHY is POR QUÉ   (POR KAY)
Imagine asking your mother "WHY PORK for tea again?"

○ The Spanish for HOW is CÓMO   (KOMO)
Imagine asking "HOW COME?"

○ The Spanish for WHO is QUIÉN   (KEE EN)
Imagine an ignorant person asking "WHO IS QUEEN?"

○ The Spanish for HOW MUCH is CUÁNTO   (KOO ANTO)
Imagine asking HOW MUCH it is when you
buy a large QUANTITY.

YOU CAN WRITE YOUR ANSWERS IN

- ○ What is the English for cuánto? _____
- ○ What is the English for quién? _____
- ○ What is the English for cómo? _____
- ○ What is the English for por qué? _____
- ○ What is the English for dónde? _____

TURN BACK FOR THE ANSWERS

COVER UP THE LEFT HAND PAGE BEFORE ANSWERING

○ What is the Spanish for how much? _____

○ What is the Spanish for who? _____

○ What is the Spanish for how? _____

○ What is the Spanish for why? _____

○ What is the Spanish for where? _____

TURN BACK FOR THE ANSWERS

ELEMENTARY GRAMMAR

When you ask questions using words like WHERE, or WHY, you ask a question in the same way as in English.

For example:

¿POR QUÉ QUIERE UN ELEFANTE?	is	WHY DOES HE WANT AN ELEPHANT?
¿DÓNDE ESTÁ EL MERCADO?	is	WHERE IS THE MARKET?
¿CÓMO COME EL ELEFANTE?	is	HOW DOES HE (or SHE) EAT THE ELPHANT?
¿QUIÉN ES LA MUCHACHA?	is	WHO IS THE GIRL?

When you want to say YOU (for example, YOU EAT) in Spanish, you do not need the word for YOU.

So, in Spanish, YOU EAT is the same as EATS (COME).

YOU WANT is WANTS (QUIERE)

YOU HAVE is HAS (TIENE)

Remember that you also do not need the words for HE, SHE, IT, etc.

Now cover up the answers below and translate the following:

(You can write your answers in)

1. WHO IS THE OWNER?
2. WHERE IS THE MANAGER?
3. WHY IS THE ELEPHANT QUICK?
4. HOW DO YOU WANT THE DUCK?
5. HOW MUCH MONEY HAS HE?

The answers are:

1. ¿QUIÉN ES EL PROPIETARIO?
2. ¿DÓNDE ESTÁ EL DIRECTOR?
3. ¿POR QUÉ EL ELEFANTE ESTÁ RÁPIDO?
4. ¿CÓMO QUIERE EL PATO?
5. ¿CUÁNTO DINERO TIENE?

Now cover up the answers below and translate the following:

(You can write your answers in)

1. ¿DÓNDE ESTÁN EL PROPIETARIO Y EL DIRECTOR?
2. ¿POR QUÉ LOS JEFES Y LOS DIRECTORES SON BLANCOS?
3. ¿CÓMO QUIERE (=you) LAS TIENDAS Y LAS FÁBRICAS?
4. ¿CUÁNTO ES EL SALARIO?
5. ¿POR QUÉ LOS CHEQUES Y LOS RECIBOS ESTÁN SUCIOS?

The answers are:

1. WHERE ARE THE OWNER AND THE MANAGER?
2. WHY ARE THE BOSSES AND THE MANAGERS WHITE?
3. HOW DO YOU WANT THE SHOPS AND THE FACTORIES?
4. HOW MUCH IS THE SALARY?
5. WHY ARE THE CHEQUES AND THE RECEIPTS DIRTY?

Remember the word order is not changed in Spanish when you ask a question.

Don't worry if you have made mistakes. You will be understood.

BUSINESSES AND SHOPS

THINK OF EACH IMAGE IN YOUR MIND'S EYE FOR ABOUT TEN SECONDS

○ The Spanish for BARBER'S SHOP is BARBERÍA
Imagine that the barber who is   (BARBEREE A)
cutting your hair is a BARBARIAN.

○ The Spanish for CHEMIST'S SHOP is FARMACIA
Imagine the PHARMACY in your   (FARMATHYA)
local chemist's shop.

○ The Spanish for HARDWARE SHOP is FERRETERÍA
Imagine FERRETS running wild   (FERRETEREE A)
amongst the pots and pans in a hardware shop.

○ The Spanish for LAUNDERETTE is LAVANDERÍA
Imagine someone spilling   (LAVANDEREE A)
LAVENDER water all over the launderette.

○ The Spanish for SUPERMARKET is   (SOOPER MERKADO)
SUPERMERCADO
Imagine bullfighters doing their
weekly shopping in a SUPERMARKET.

○ The Spanish for TOBACCONIST is   (TABAKEREE A)
TABAQUERÍA
Imagine a bullfighter in a
TOBACCONIST'S SHOP.

YOU CAN WRITE YOUR ANSWERS IN

○ What is the English for tabaquería? _____

○ What is the English for supermercado? _____

○ What is the English for lavandería? _____

○ What is the English for ferretería? _____

○ What is the English for farmacia? _____

○ What is the English for barbería? _____

TURN BACK FOR THE ANSWERS

YOU CAN WRITE YOUR ANSWERS IN

○ What is the Spanish for tobacconist? _____

○ What is the Spanish for supermarket? _____

○ What is the Spanish for launderette? _____

○ What is the Spanish for hardware shop? _____

○ What is the Spanish for chemist's shop? _____

○ What is the Spanish for barber's shop? _____

TURN BACK FOR THE ANSWERS

Now cover up the answers below and translate the following:

(You can write your answers in)

1. THE SUPERMARKET AND THE CHEMIST'S SHOP ARE HERE
2. THE SALESMAN WANTS A RECEIPT AND THE MONEY
3. THE ACCOUNTANT HAS A JOB IN THE OFFICE
4. THE BARBER'S SHOP AND THE LAUNDERETTE ARE GOOD BUSINESSES
5. THE MISTAKE IS HERE

The answers are:

1. EL SUPERMERCADO Y LA FARMACIA ESTÁN AQUÍ
2. EL VENDEDOR QUIERE UN RECIBO Y EL DINERO
3. EL CONTADOR TIENE UN EMPLEO EN LA OFICINA
4. LA BARBERÍA Y LA LAVANDERÍA SON BUENOS NEGOCIOS
   (N.B. GOOD often comes before the noun)
5. EL ERROR ESTÁ AQUÍ

Now cover up the answers below and translate the following:

(You can write your answers in)

1. LAS VACACIONES ESTÁN AQUÍ Y NO ALLÁ
2. LOS PRODUCTOS SON MUY BUENOS
3. EL PRECIO ES SIEMPRE ALTO
4. LA FERRETERÍA TIENE COSAS CARAS
5. LA PRIMERA TIENDA ES MUY LARGA

The answers are:

1. THE HOLIDAYS ARE HERE AND NOT THERE
2. THE PRODUCTS ARE VERY GOOD
3. THE PRICE IS ALWAYS HIGH
4. THE HARDWARE SHOP HAS EXPENSIVE THINGS
5. THE FIRST SHOP IS VERY LONG

Section 8 TRAVELLING, THE CAR

TRAVELLING AND ARRIVING AT YOUR DESTINATION

THINK OF EACH IMAGE IN YOUR MIND'S EYE FOR ABOUT TEN SECONDS

○ The Spanish for PASSPORT is PASAPORTE
Imagine a bullfighter stamping your   (PASAPORTAY)
PASSPORT when you arrive in Spain.

○ The Spanish for SUITCASE is MALETA   (MALETA)
Imagine MY LETTER is in your suitcase.

○ The Spanish for CUSTOMS is ADUANA   (ADOO ANA)
Imagine going through the customs saying
"ADD ONE. Add two", etc.

○ The Spanish for TOILET is RETRETE   (RETRETAY)
Imagine RETREATING to the toilet.

○ The Spanish for TICKET is BILLETE   (BEELYETAY)
Imagine thinking "I will BE LATE if I don't find my tickets."

○ The Spanish for DANGER is PELIGRO   (PELEEGRO)
Imagine someone shouting "Danger, don't
eat that, it will make your BELLY GROW."

○ The Spanish for GENTLEMEN is SEÑORES
Imagine a number of SENIOR men   (SENYORAYS)
entering the gentlemen's toilet.

○ The Spanish for LADIES is SEÑORAS   (SENYORAS)
Imagine a number of SENIOR ladies
entering the ladies' toilet.

○ The Spanish for ENTRANCE is ENTRADA   (ENTRADA)
Imagine a bullfighter ENTERING A bullring.

○ The Spanish for EXIT is SALIDA   (SALEEDA)
Imagine SALAD spread all over the exit to your hotel.

YOU CAN WRITE YOUR ANSWERS IN

○ What is the English for salida? _____

○ What is the English for entrada? _____

○ What is the English for señoras? _____

○ What is the English for señores? _____

○ What is the English for peligro? _____

○ What is the English for billete? _____

○ What is the English for retrete? _____

○ What is the English for aduana? _____

○ What is the English for maleta? _____

○ What is the English for pasaporte? _____

TURN BACK FOR THE ANSWERS

COVER UP THE LEFT HAND SIDE BEFORE ANSWERING

○ What is the Spanish for exit? ＿＿＿＿＿＿

○ What is the Spanish for entrance? ＿＿＿＿＿＿

○ What is the Spanish for ladies? ＿＿＿＿＿＿

○ What is the Spanish for gentlemen? ＿＿＿＿＿＿

○ What is the Spanish for danger? ＿＿＿＿＿＿

○ What is the Spanish for ticket? ＿＿＿＿＿＿

○ What is the Spanish for toilet? ＿＿＿＿＿＿

○ What is the Spanish for customs? ＿＿＿＿＿＿

○ What is the Spanish for suitcase? ＿＿＿＿＿＿

○ What is the Spanish for passport? ＿＿＿＿＿＿

TURN BACK FOR THE ANSWERS

THINK OF EACH IMAGE IN YOUR MIND'S EYE FOR ABOUT TEN SECONDS

○ The Spanish for BOAT is BARCO   (BARKO)
Imagine a dog BARKING as you embark on a boat.

○ The Spanish for CAR is COCHE   (KOCHAY)
Imagine your car is converted into an old-fashioned COACH.

○ The Spanish for BUS is AUTOBÚS   (A OOTOBOOS)
Imagine A BUS filled with bullfighters.

○ The Spanish for TRAIN is TREN   (TREN)
Imagine bullfighters leaning out of TRAIN carriages.

○ The Spanish for GARAGE is GARAJE   (GARAHAY)
Imagine a bullfighter serving petrol on the
forecourt of a GARAGE.

○ The Spanish for PETROL is GASOLINA   (GASOLEENA)
Imagine filling your car with GAS instead of petrol.

○ The Spanish for OIL is ACEITE   (ATHE EETAY)
Imagine oil being so ACIDY that it burns
a hole when you drop some.

○ The Spanish for PUNCTURE is PINCHAZO
Imagine when a lady bends down to   (PEENCHATHO)
inspect a puncture you PINCH HER,
THOUGH we're not saying where!

○ The Spanish for WHEEL is RUEDA   (ROO EDA)
Imagine little wheels appearing on a RADAR screen.

○ The Spanish for JACK is GATO   (GATO)
Imagine using a sponge GATEAU as a jack.
(It's the same as for CAT.)

YOU CAN WRITE YOUR ANSWERS IN

○ What is the English for gato? _____

○ What is the English for rueda? _____

○ What is the English for pinchazo? _____

○ What is the English for aceite? _____

○ What is the English for gasolina? _____

○ What is the English for garaje? _____

○ What is the English for tren? _____

○ What is the English for autobús? _____

○ What is the English for coche? _____

○ What is the English for barco? _____

TURN BACK FOR THE ANSWERS

COVER UP THE LEFT HAND PAGE BEFORE ANSWERING

○ What is the Spanish for jack?   _____

○ What is the Spanish for wheel?   _____

○ What is the Spanish for puncture?   _____

○ What is the Spanish for oil?   _____

○ What is the Spanish for petrol?   _____

○ What is the Spanish for garage?   _____

○ What is the Spanish for train?   _____

○ What is the Spanish for bus?   _____

○ What is the Spanish for car?   _____

○ What is the Spanish for boat?   _____

TURN BACK FOR THE ANSWERS

ELEMENTARY GRAMMAR

You will remember that the Spanish for

    EATS   is COME
    HAS   is TIENE
    WANTS is QUIERE

The Spanish for I WANT is QUIERO (pronounced KEE ERO)
The Spanish for I EAT   is COMO (pronounced KOMO)
The Spanish for I HAVE is TENGO (pronounced TENGO)

Remember that I means "O" at the end of the word.

So,

    I HAVE A TICKET is TENGO UN BILLETE

Note that in Spanish I WANT and I AM WANTING, I EAT and I
AM EATING, etc., are the same.

Now cover up the answers below and translate the following:

(Your can write your answers in)

1. I HAVE A TICKET
2. I WANT THE CUSTOMS
3. I AM EATING THE PIG
4. HE IS THE BOSS
5. I HAVE A BOAT AND A CAR

The answers are:

1. TENGO UN BILLETE
2. QUIERO LA ADUANA
3. COMO EL PUERCO
4. ES EL JEFE
5. TENGO UN BARCO Y UN COCHE

Now cover up the answers below and translate the following:

(You can write your answers in)

1. ES EL PROPIETARIO
2. TENGO UN PASAPORTE Y UNA MALETA
3. COMO EL BILLETE, Y EL PERRO COME LA RUEDA
4. QUIERO UN GARAJE
5. ES UN CONTADOR

The answers are:

1. HE IS THE OWNER (or YOU ARE THE OWNER)
2. I HAVE A PASSPORT AND A SUITCASE
3. I AM EATING THE TICKET, AND THE DOG IS EATING THE WHEEL
4. I WANT A GARAGE
5. HE IS AN ACCOUNTANT (or YOU ARE AN ACCOUNTANT)

ELEMENTARY GRAMMAR

The next elementary **grammar** point is about the word for I AM.

In Spanish the phrase I AM is ESTOY if the state is temporary or SOY if it is permanent.

For example:

PERMANENT STATE	*TEMPORARY STATE*
I AM A PIG	I AM QUICK
SOY UN PUERCO	ESTOY RÁPIDO
I AM A DOG	I AM FRESH
SOY UN PERRO	ESTOY FRESCO
I AM THE MANAGER	I AM FREE
SOY EL DIRECTOR	ESTOY LIBRE

In an earlier section you learned that the word for NO is NO, and it is also the word for not.

To say THE CAR IS NOT SMALL, you simply say THE CAR NOT IS SMALL

(EL COCHE NO ES PEQUEÑO)

In other words, you put the NO before the verb.

So,

THE DOG IS NOT QUICK is EL PERRO NO ESTÁ RÁPIDO

There is one important rule to remember: the word for A is usually omitted when you use the word NO.

For example:

I DO NOT HAVE A COW is NO TENGO VACA

(Remember "I" is also missed out in Spanish.)

YOU DO NOT HAVE A BULL is NO TIENE TORO
YOU DO NOT EAT PIGS   is NO COME PUERCOS
I AM A DOG   is SOY UN PERRO
I AM NOT A DOG   is NO SOY PERRO

With the word THE, EL or LA are left in.

I AM NOT THE PIG is NO SOY EL PUERCO

Now cover up the answers below and translate the following:

(You can write your answers in)

1. IT IS NOT A CAR
2. HE IS NOT A DUCK
3. I AM NOT THE OWNER
4. I HAVE A PASSPORT
5. IT IS NOT A SUITCASE

The answers are:

1. NO ES COCHE
2. NO ES PATO
3. NO SOY EL PROPIETARIO
4. TENGO UN PASAPORTE
5. NO ES MALETA

Now cover up the answers below and translate the following:

(You can write your answers in)

1. ESTOY SUCIO. EL RETRETE ESTÁ AQUÍ

2. SOY PEQUEÑO, PERO COMO UN CABALLO

3. LA CAMA ES DURA Y VIEJA

4. TENGO UNA MALETA AMARILLA, Y LA MUCHACHA TIENE UNA MALETA AZUL

5. SOY UN MARIDO, Y QUIERO SOPA O LECHE Y AZÚCAR

The answers are:

1. I AM DIRTY. THE TOILET IS HERE

2. I AM SMALL, BUT I EAT A HORSE

3. THE BED IS HARD AND OLD

4. I HAVE A YELLOW SUITCASE, AND THE GIRL HAS A BLUE SUITCASE

5. I AM A HUSBAND, AND I WANT SOUP OR MILK AND SUGAR

SOME MORE TRAVELLING WORDS

THINK OF EACH IMAGE IN YOUR MIND'S EYE FOR ABOUT TEN SECONDS

○ The Spanish for TYRE is NEUMÁTICO (NE OOMATEEKO)
Imagine blowing up a PNEUMATIC tyre.

○ The Spanish for EXHAUST is ESCAPE (ESKAPAY)
Imagine exhaust fumes ESCAPING from a car.

○ The Spanish for MAP is (EL) MAPA (MAPA)
Imagine a bullfighter studying a MAP.

○ The Spanish for PUMP is BOMBA (BOMBA)
Imagine a BOMB On your pump, which
explodes when the pump is switched on.

○ The Spanish for KEY is (LA) LLAVE (LYAVAY)
Imagine that you have left your key in the LAVATORY.

○ The Spanish for ENGINE is MOTOR (MOTOR)
Imagine your MOTOR car won't start
because the engine has broken down.

○ The Spanish for DRIVER is CONDUCTOR (KONDOOKTOR)
Imagine the driver of your car is a bus CONDUCTOR.

○ The Spanish for FAN is VENTILADOR (VENTEELADOR)
Imagine you use a fan for a
VENTILATOR for your car.

○ The Spanish for SEAT is ASIENTO (ASEE ENTO)
Imagine you have to ASCEND TO sit on your seat.

○ The Spanish for TANK is DEPÓSITO (DEPOSEETO)
Imagine you DEPOSIT petrol in your tank.

YOU CAN WRITE YOUR ANSWERS IN

○ What is the English for depósito?   _____

○ What is the English for asiento?   _____

○ What is the English for ventilador?   _____

○ What is the English for conductor?   _____

○ What is the English for motor?   _____

○ What is the English for (la) llave?   _____

○ What is the English for bomba?   _____

○ What is the English for (el) mapa?   _____

○ What is the English for escape?   _____

○ What is the English for neumático?   _____

TURN BACK FOR THE ANSWERS

COVER UP THE LEFT HAND PAGE BEFORE ANSWERING

○ What is the Spanish for tank? _____

○ What is the Spanish for seat? _____

○ What is the Spanish for fan? _____

○ What is the Spanish for driver? _____

○ What is the Spanish for engine? _____

○ What is the Spanish for key? _____

○ What is the Spanish for pump? _____

○ What is the Spanish for map? _____

○ What is the Spanish for exhaust? _____

○ What is the Spanish for tyre? _____

TURN BACK FOR THE ANSWERS

ELEMENTARY GRAMMAR

The Spanish for SOME is UNOS or UNAS.

UNOS is MASCULINE
UNAS is FEMININE

So,

TENGO UNAS VACAS is I HAVE SOME COWS
COMO UNOS TOROS   is I EAT SOME BULLS

Now cover up the answers below and translate the following:

(You can write your answers in)

1. I HAVE SOME TICKETS
2. I EAT SOME CATS
3. I WANT SOME WHEELS
4. SHE HAS SOME TABLES
5. IT HAS SOME GEESE

The answers are:

1. TENGO UNOS BILLETES
2. COMO UNOS GATOS
3. QUIERO UNAS RUEDAS
4. TIENE UNAS MESAS
5. TIENE UNOS GANSOS

Now cover up the answers below and translate the following:

(You can write your answers in)

1. NO ES ENTRADA Y NO ES SALIDA
2. QUIERE (=he) UNOS PASAPORTES PERO NO EL BILLETE
3. NO, NO ES LA ADUANA
4. LOS SEÑORES Y LAS SEÑORAS ESTÁN AQUÍ
5. EL AUTOBÚS, EL COCHE Y EL TREN ESTÁN EN EL GARAJE

The answers are:

1. IT IS NOT AN ENTRANCE AND IT IS NOT AN EXIT
2. HE WANTS SOME PASSPORTS BUT NOT THE TICKET
3. NO, IT IS NOT THE CUSTOMS
4. THE GENTLEMEN AND THE LADIES ARE HERE
5. THE BUS, THE CAR AND THE TRAIN ARE IN THE GARAGE

ELEMENTARY GRAMMAR

To say you have NOT got some cows, or tables, and so on, you leave out the UNOS and UNAS.

NO TENGO MALETAS is I DO NOT HAVE (ANY) SUITCASES

NO COMO PATOS   is I DO NOT EAT (ANY) DUCKS

Now cover up the answers below and translate the following:

(You can write your answers in)

1. YOU DO NOT WANT (ANY) TICKETS
2. HE DOES NOT EAT (ANY) PLATES
3. YOU DO NOT HAVE (ANY) PASSPORTS
4. SHE HAS SOME CARS
5. I DO NOT HAVE (ANY) SUITCASES

The answers are:

1. NO QUIERE BILLETES
2. NO COME PLATOS
3. NO TIENE PASAPORTES
4. TIENE UNOS COCHES
5. NO TENGO MALETAS

Now cover up the answers below and translate the following:

(You can write your answers in)

1. ES UN PINCHAZO PERO NO TENGO GATO
2. EL CONDUCTOR QUIERE GASOLINA Y ACEITE EN EL DEPÓSITO
3. LOS NEUMÁTICOS SON MUY VIEJOS
4. NO QUIERO RUEDAS, NO QUIERO BOMBAS PERO QUIERO UNOS ASIENTOS Y UNOS VENTILADORES
5. NO TENGO BARCOS AMARILLOS

The answers are:

1. IT IS A PUNCTURE BUT I DO NOT HAVE A JACK
2. THE DRIVER WANTS PETROL AND OIL IN THE TANK
3. THE TYRES ARE VERY OLD
4. I DO NOT WANT (ANY) WHEELS, I DO NOT WANT (ANY) PUMPS, BUT I WANT SOME SEATS AND SOME FANS
5. I DO NOT HAVE (ANY) YELLOW BOATS

Section 9 ON BEACH AND LEISURE ACTIVITIES

THINK OF EACH IMAGE IN YOUR MIND'S EYE FOR ABOUT TEN SECONDS

○ The Spanish for BEACH is PLAYA   (PLAYA)
Imagine PLIERS scattered all over the beach.

○ The Spanish for SAND is ARENA   (ARENA)
Imagine clowns in a circus ARENA
throwing sand at each other.

○ The Spanish for DECKCHAIR is HAMACA   (AMAKA)
Imagine a HAMMOCK slung between two deckchairs

○ The Spanish for PICNIC is MERIENDA   (MEREE ENDA)
Imagine your picnic coming to a MERRY END,
possibly because people have drunk too much.

○ The Spanish for SUN is SOL   (SOL)
Imagine SAUL in the Bible, staring at the sun.

○ The Spanish for COLD is FRÍO   (FREE O)
Imagine being FREEzing cold.

○ The Spanish for HEAT is CALOR   (KALOR)
Imagine using CALOR gas to heat something up.

○ The Spanish for (TO) RESCUE is SALVAR   (SALVAR)
Imagine giving someone a silver SALVER
after they have rescued you.

○ The Spanish for SEA is MAR   (MAR)
Imagine yelling "MA! get me out of the sea."

○ The Spanish for ROCK is ROCA   (ROKA)
Imagine a bullfighter standing on some ROCKS.

YOU CAN WRITE YOUR ANSWERS IN

○ What is the English for roca? _____

○ What is the English for mar? _____

○ What is the English for salvar? _____

○ What is the English for calor? _____

○ What is the English for frío? _____

○ What is the English for sol? _____

○ What is the English for merienda? _____

○ What is the English for hamaca? _____

○ What is the English for arena? _____

○ What is the English for playa? _____

TURN BACK FOR THE ANSWERS

COVER UP THE LEFT HAND PAGE BEFORE ANSWERING

○ What is the Spanish for rock?   _____

○ What is the Spanish for sea?   _____

○ What is the Spanish for to rescue?   _____

○ What is the Spanish for heat?   _____

○ What is the Spanish for cold?   _____

○ What is the Spanish for sun?   _____

○ What is the Spanish for picnic?   _____

○ What is the Spanish for deckchair?   _____

○ What is the Spanish for sand?   _____

○ What is the Spanish for beach?   _____

TURN BACK FOR THE ANSWERS

ELEMENTARY GRAMMAR

Here are some useful words:

The Spanish for MY is MI (pronounced MEE)

Imagine thinking "Give ME MY car."

The Spanish for YOUR, HIS, HER and ITS is SU (pronounced SOO)

Imagine thinking, I will SUE your, his, her, its family for damages.

So,

MY BULL	is	MI TORO
MY COW	is	MI VACA
YOUR BEACH	is	SU PLAYA

HIS or HER BEACH is also SU PLAYA
ITS (or HIS or HER or YOUR) PICNIC is SU MERIENDA

The Spanish for MY and YOUR when the noun is plural is MIS or SUS. In other words, you add an S.

So,

MY COWS	is	MIS VACAS
MY TOILETS	is	MIS RETRETES
MY BEACHES	is	MIS PLAYAS
YOUR DECKCHAIRS	is	SUS HAMACAS
YOUR PICNICS	is	SUS MERIENDAS

LEISURE ACTIVITIES

THINK OF EACH IMAGE IN YOUR MIND'S EYE FOR
ABOUT TEN SECONDS

○ The Spanish for PARTY is FIESTA   (FEE ESTA)
    Imagine having a FEAST in the middle of your party.

○ The Spanish for BULLFIGHT is CORRIDA   (KORREEDA)
    Imagine having a bullfight in a CORRIDOR.

○ The Spanish for LAKE is LAGO   (LAGO)
    Imagine a lake made of LAGER beer.

○ The Spanish for RIVER is RÍO   (REE O)
    Imagine a famous river, the RIO Grande.

○ The Spanish for MOUNTAIN is MONTAÑA   (MONTANYA)
    Imagine mountains in the American state of MONTANA.

○ The Spanish for STAMP is SELLO   (SELYO)
    Imagine someone who wants to SELL YOU a stamp.

○ The Spanish for ENVELOPE is SOBRE   (SOBRAY)
    Imagine being SOBER enough, just, to stick
    down an envelope.

○ The Spanish for LETTER is CARTA   (KARTA)
    Imagine Ex-President Jimmy CARTER
    reading a letter.

○ The Spanish for PEN is PLUMA   (PLOOMA)
    Imagine PLUMAge sticking out of your pen.

○ The Spanish for BOOK is LIBRO   (LEEBRO)
    Imagine a LIBRARY with books.

YOU CAN WRITE YOUR ANSWERS IN

○ What is the English for libro? _____

○ What is the English for pluma? _____

○ What is the English for carta? _____

○ What is the English for sobre? _____

○ What is the English for sello? _____

○ What is the English for montana? _____

○ What is the English for río? _____

○ What is the English for lago? _____

○ What is the English for corrida? _____

○ What is the English for fiesta? _____

TURN BACK FOR THE ANSWERS

YOU CAN WRITE YOUR ANSWERS IN

○ What is the Spanish for book? _____

○ What is the Spanish for pen? _____

○ What is the Spanish for letter? _____

○ What is the Spanish for envelope? _____

○ What is the Spanish for stamp? _____

○ What is the Spanish for mountain? _____

○ What is the Spanish for river? _____

○ What is the Spanish for lake? _____

○ What is the Spanish for bullfight? _____

○ What is the Spanish for party? _____

TURN BACK FOR THE ANSWERS

Now cover up the answers below and translate the following:

(You can write your answers in)

1. I AM YOUR BOY
2. I AM HIS BROTHER
3. IT IS MY PIG
4. IT IS MY BEACH
5. IT IS MY SUN

The answers are:

1. SOY SU MUCHACHO
2. SOY SU HERMANO
3. ES MI PUERCO
4. ES MI PLAYA
5. ES MI SOL

Now cover up the answers below and translate the following:

(You can write your answers in)

1. LA ARENA ESTÁ EN SUS HAMACAS Y ESTÁ EN MIS CARTAS

2. ES SU SOBRE, Y MI SELLA

3. QUIERO SUS MONTANAS Y SUS RÍOS

4. ¡PELIGRO! SU FIESTA ESTÁ MUY TRANQUILA

5. EL AGUA ESTÁ FRÍA HOY PERO LA MERIENDA ESTÁ AQUÍ EN UN BARCO EN EL LAGO

The answers are:

1. THE SAND IS ON YOUR (or HIS, HER) DECKCHAIRS AND IS ON (or IN) MY LETTERS

2. IT IS YOUR (or HIS, HER, ITS) ENVELOPE, AND MY STAMP

3. I WANT YOUR (or HIS, HER, ITS) MOUNTAINS AND YOUR (or HIS, HER, ITS) RIVERS

4. DANGER! YOUR (or HIS, HER, ITS) PARTY IS VERY QUIET

5. THE WATER IS COLD TODAY, BUT THE PICNIC IS HERE ON (or IN) A BOAT ON (or IN) THE LAKE

Remember:

SU can be YOUR or HIS or HER or ITS

SOME MORE USEFUL WORDS

THINK OF EACH IMAGE IN YOUR MIND'S EYE FOR ABOUT TEN SECONDS

○ The Spanish for DOCTOR is MÉDICO   (MEDEEKO)
Imagine your doctor with bottles of MEDICINE.

○ The Spanish for DENTIST is (EL) DENTISTA
Imagine a bullfighter at the DENTIST'S.   (DENTEESTA)

○ The Spanish for LAWYER is ABOGADO   (ABOGADO)
Imagine a lawyer eating an AVOCADO
pear in the middle of the defence of his client.

○ The Spanish for POLICE is POLICÍA   (POLEETHEE A)
Imagine the POLICE arresting a bullfighter.

○ The Spanish for BANK is BANCO   (BANKO)
Imagine your BANK filled with bullfighters.

○ The Spanish for HOTEL is HOTEL   (OTEL)
Imagine a bullfighter's convention at your HOTEL.

○ The Spanish for POST OFFICE is CORREO   (KORREO)
Imagine a post office in KOREA, with
Korean signs outside.

○ The Spanish for CAMPING SITE is CAMPING
Imagine bullfighters CAMPING at a   (CAMPEENG)
camping site.

○ The Spanish for ROAD is CARRETERA   (KARRETERA)
Imagine CARROTS strewn all over the road.

○ The Spanish for MUSEUM is MUSEO   (MOOSEO)
Imagine an exhibition of bullfighters at
your local MUSEUM.

YOU CAN WRITE YOUR ANSWERS IN

○ What is the English for museo? _____

○ What is the English for carretera? _____

○ What is the English for camping? _____

○ What is the English for correo? _____

○ What is the English for hotel? _____

○ What is the English for banco? _____

○ What is the English for policía? _____

○ What is the English for (el) abogado? _____

○ What is the English for (el) dentista? _____

○ What is the English for médico? _____

TURN BACK FOR THE ANSWERS

COVER UP THE LEFT HAND PAGE BEFORE ANSWERING

○ What is the Spanish for museum? _____

○ What is the Spanish for road? _____

○ What is the Spanish for camping site? _____

○ What is the Spanish for post office? _____

○ What is the Spanish for hotel? _____

○ What is the Spanish for bank? _____

○ What is the Spanish for police? _____

○ What is the Spanish for lawyer? _____

○ What is the Spanish for dentist? _____

○ What is the Spanish for doctor? _____

TURN BACK FOR THE ANSWERS

Now cover up the answers below and translate the following:

(You can write your answers in)

1. THE HEAT IS HERE TODAY

2. THE SEA AND THE ROCK WERE HERE, BUT THE ROAD
   AND THE MUSEUM ARE NOT HERE

3. THE BULLFIGHT WAS IN THE HOTEL

4. YOUR DOCTOR WANTS MORE MONEY AND MY
   DENTIST WANTS MORE CHEESE

5. MY DOGS WERE UNDER A BANK

The answers are:

1. EL CALOR ESTÁ AQUÍ HOY

2. EL MAR Y LA ROCA ESTABAN AQUÍ, PERO LA
   CARRETERA Y EL MUSEO NO ESTÁN AQUÍ

3. LA CORRIDA ESTABA EN EL HOTEL

4. SU MÉDICO QUIERE MÁS DINERO Y MI DENTISTA
   QUIERE MÁS QUESO

5. MIS PERROS ESTABAN DEBAJO DE UN BANCO

Now cover up the answers below and translate the following:

(You can write your answers in)

1. LA PLUMA Y EL LIBRO ESTÁN EN LA MESA
2. MIS ABOGADOS ESTÁN FUERA DE UN GUARDARROPA
3. LA LLAVE Y EL MAPA ESTABAN EN LA CARRETERA
4. MI MOTOR Y MI ESCAPE SON MUY VIEJOS
5. EL CAMPING Y EL CORREO TIENEN FLORES AZULES

The answers are:

1. THE PEN AND THE BOOK ARE ON THE TABLE
2. MY LAWYERS ARE OUTSIDE A CLOAKROOM
3. THE KEY AND THE MAP WERE ON THE ROAD
4. MY ENGINE AND MY EXHAUST ARE VERY OLD
5. THE CAMPING SITE AND THE POST OFFICE HAVE BLUE FLOWERS

PLEASE NOTE:

Plurals

Verbs in sentences such as the previous sentence
   (THE CAMPING SITE AND THE POST OFFICE HAVE ...)

or THEY HAVE, or THEY EAT, etc., always end in "N".

So,

The camping site and the post office HAVE ... is
El camping y el correo TIENEN ...

Section 10 AT THE DOCTORS, EMERGENCY WORDS, USEFUL WORDS

ILLNESS

THINK OF EACH IMAGE IN YOUR MIND'S EYE FOR ABOUT TEN SECONDS

○ The Spanish for PAIN is DOLOR   (DOLOR)
Imagine being given a DOLLAR to make your pain go away.

○ The Spanish for ILL is ENFERMO   (ENFERMO)
Imagine being ill and INFIRM.

○ The Spanish for COUGH is (LA) TOS   (TOS)
Imagine you cough in the middle of TOSSING
a coin, and drop the coin.

○ The Spanish for ARM is BRAZO   (BRATHO)
Imagine BRASS bracelets wrapped around your arm.

○ The Spanish for EYE is OJO   (OHO)
Imagine the doctor saying "OH HO!" as he
pokes you in the eye.

○ The Spanish for FACE is CARA   (KARA)
Imagine your face looking as if a CAR HAD hit it.

○ The Spanish for HAND is (LA) MANO   (MANO)
Imagine dropping someone's hand down a MANHOLE.

○ The Spanish for SKIN is (LA) PIEL   (PEE EL)
Imagine your skin beginning to PEEL in the sun.

○ The Spanish for BLOOD is (LA) SANGRE   (SANGRAY)
Imagine being SO ANGRY that you draw blood.

○ The Spanish for MOUTH is (LA) BOCA   (BOKA)
Imagine A POKER sticking out of someone's mouth.

YOU CAN WRITE YOUR ANSWERS IN

○ What is the English for boca? _____

○ What is the English for (la) sangre? _____

○ What is the English for (la) piel? _____

○ What is the English for (la) mano? _____

○ What is the English for cara? _____

○ What is the English for ojo? _____

○ What is the English for brazo? _____

○ What is the English for (la) tos? _____

○ What is the English for enfermo? _____

○ What is the English for dolor? _____

TURN BACK FOR THE ANSWERS

COVER UP THE LEFT HAND PAGE BEFORE ANSWERING

○ What is the Spanish for mouth?   _____

○ What is the Spanish for blood?   _____

○ What is the Spanish for skin?   _____

○ What is the Spanish for hand?   _____

○ What is the Spanish for face?   _____

○ What is the Spanish for eye?   _____

○ What is the Spanish for arm?   _____

○ What is the Spanish for cough?   _____

○ What is the Spanish for ill?   _____

○ What is the Spanish for pain?   _____

TURN BACK FOR THE ANSWERS

EMERGENCY AND USEFUL WORDS

THINK OF EACH IMAGE IN YOUR MIND'S EYE FOR ABOUT TEN SECONDS

○ The Spanish for HOSPITAL is HOSPITAL   (OSPEETAL)
Imagine a bullfighter being carted off to HOSPITAL.

○ The Spanish for BANDAGE is VENDA   (VENDA)
Imagine you BEND A bandage
backwards and forwards to get it off.

○ The Spanish for AMBULANCE is   (AMBULANTHYA)
AMBULANCIA
Imagine bullfighter being loaded into an AMBULANCE.

○ The Spanish for ACCIDENT is   (AKTHEEDENTAY)
ACCIDENTE
Imagine a bullfighter in a nasty ACCIDENT.

○ The Spanish for THIEF is LADRÓN   (LADRON)
Imagine a thief disappearing down the
street with a LADDER ON his back.

○ The Spanish for FIRE is FUEGO   (FOO EGO)
Imagine telling the hotel manager
"IF WE GO there will be a fire."

○ The Spanish for DEAD is MUERTO   (MOO ERTO)
Imagine telling someone that he was
MORTAL, that is why he is now dead.

○ The Spanish for STREET is (LA) CALLE   (KALYAY)
Imagine you hear someone CALL YOU in the street.

○ The Spanish for HELP is AYUDA   (AYOODA)
Imagine shouting "HEY YOU THERE, help!"

○ The Spanish for TELEPHONE is TELÉFONO   (TELEFONO)
Imagine a bullfighter using a TELEPHONE.

YOU CAN WRITE YOUR ANSWERS IN

○ What is the English for teléfono? _____

○ What is the English for ayuda? _____

○ What is the English for (la) calle? _____

○ What is the English for muerto? _____

○ What is the English for fuego? _____

○ What is the English for ladrón? _____

○ What is the Enlish for accidente? _____

○ What is the English for ambulancia? _____

○ What is the English for venda? _____

○ What is the English for hospital? _____

TURN BACK FOR THE ANSWERS

COVER UP THE LEFT HAND PAGE BEFORE ANSWERING

O What is the Spanish for telephone?   _____

O What is the Spanish for help?   _____

O What is the Spanish for street?   _____

O What is the Spanish for dead?   _____

O What is the Spanish for fire?   _____

O What is the Spanish for thief?   _____

O What is the Spanish for accident?   _____

O What is the Spanish for ambulance?   _____

O What is the Spanish for bandage?   _____

O What is the Spanish for hospital?   _____

TURN BACK FOR THE ANSWERS

MORE USEFUL WORDS

THINK OF EACH IMAGE IN YOUR MIND'S EYE FOR ABOUT TEN SECONDS

○ The Spanish for THANK YOU is GRACIAS   (GRATHYAS)
Imagine someone being GRACIOUS and
saying THANK YOU.

○ The Spanish for PLEASE is POR FAVOR   (POR FAVOR)
Imagine thinking "PLEASE POUR
FAVOURS in my direction."

○ The Spanish for SORRY is PERDONE   (PERDONAY)
Imagine saying "PARDON, I am SORRY."

○ The Spanish for HELLO is HOLÁ   (OLA)
Imagine saying "HELLO" to someone who is
practising with a HOOLA-hoop.

○ The Spanish for GOOD-BYE is ADIÓS   (ADYOS)
Imagine thinking "GOOD-BYE IDIOTS!"

○ The Spanish for BEFORE is ANTES DE   (ANTES DAY)
Imagine it is your AUNTIE'S DAY BEFORE long.

○ The Spanish for EMPTY is VACÍO   (VATHEE O)
Imagine thinking "How can I BATH YOU if
the bath is EMPTY?"

○ The Spanish for ENGAGED is OCUPADO   (OKOOPADO)
Imagine a toilet being OCCUPIED and
therefore ENGAGED.

YOU CAN WRITE YOUR ANSWERS IN

○ What is the English for ocupado?   _____

○ What is the English for vacío?   _____

○ What is the English for antes?   _____

○ What is the English for adiós?   _____

○ What is the English for holá?   _____

○ What is the English for perdone?   _____

○ What is the English for por favor?   _____

○ What is the English for gracias?   _____

TURN BACK FOR THE ANSWERS

COVER UP THE LEFT HAND PAGE BEFORE ANSWERING

○ What is the Spanish for engaged? _____

○ What is the Spanish for empty? _____

○ What is the Spanish for before? _____

○ What is the Spanish for goodbye? _____

○ What is the Spanish for hello? _____

○ What is the Spanish for sorry? _____

○ What is the Spanish for please? _____

○ What is the Spanish for thank you? _____

TURN BACK FOR THE ANSWERS

Now cover up the answers below and translate the following:

(You can write your answers in)

1. PLEASE DOCTOR, THE PAIN IS VERY BAD

2. MY EYES AND MY SKIN ARE BLACK

3. THANK YOU GENTLEMEN, THE HOSPITAL IS ALWAYS GOOD

4. HELLO, I WANT A BANDAGE BEFORE A DOG

5. SORRY, THE TELEPHONE IS NOT HERE

The answers are:

1. POR FAVOR, MÉDICO, EL DOLOR ESTÁ MUY MALO

2. MIS OJOS Y MI PIEL SON NEGROS

3. GRACIAS SEÑORES, EL HOSPITAL ES SIEMPRE BUENO

4. HOLÁ, QUIERO UNA VENDA ANTES DE UN PERRO

5. PERDONE, EL TELÉFONO NO ESTÁ AQUÍ

Now cover up the answers below and translate the following:

(You can write your answers in)

1. SU CARA ES BONITA, PERO SU VESTIDO ES VIEJO
2. LA MANO ESTÁ VACÍA
3. LA SANGRE ESTÁ EN EL BRAZO Y EN LA BOCA
4. EL LADRÓN QUIERE UN FUEGO
5. ES UN ACCIDENTE Y UNA AMBULANCIA ESTÁ AQUÍ

The answers are:

1. YOUR (or HIS, HER, ITS) FACE IS PRETTY, BUT YOUR (or HIS, HER, ITS) DRESS IS OLD
2. THE HAND IS EMPTY
3. THE BLOOD IS ON (or IN) THE ARM AND ON (or IN) THE MOUTH
4. THE THIEF WANTS A FIRE
5. IT IS AN ACCIDENT AND AN AMBULANCE IS HERE

SOME MORE USEFUL VERBS

THINK OF EACH IMAGE IN YOUR MIND'S EYE FOR ABOUT TEN SECONDS

○ The Spanish for I SPEAK is HABLO   (ABLO)
   Imagine when I SPEAK, I BLOW.

○ The Spanish for I LIVE is VIVO   (VEEVO)
   Imagine an "in VIVO" experiment in a real-LIFE situation.

○ The Spanish for I SELL is VENDO   (VENDO)
   Imagine a street VENDOR who SELLs you something.

YOU CAN WRITE YOUR ANSWERS IN

○ What is the English for vendo? _____

○ What is the English for vivo? _____

○ What is the English for hablo? _____

TURN BACK FOR THE ANSWERS

YOU CAN WRITE YOUR ANSWERS IN

○ What is the Spanish for I sell?   _____

○ What is the Spanish for I live?   _____

○ What is the Spanish for I speak?   _____

TURN BACK FOR THE ANSWERS

ELEMENTARY GRAMMAR

Almost any adjective like EMPTY or QUICK can be made into an adverb:

EMPTILY or QUICKLY

simply by adding MENTE (pronounced MENTAY) on to the end of the word in the feminine form.

So,

HE EATS QUICKLY is COME RÁPIDAMENTE

I LIVE QUIETLY is VIVO TRANQUILAMENTE

MONTHS OF THE YEAR
The next group of words deals with the months of the year.

The Spanish for JANUARY is ENERO

(pronounced ENERO)

Imagine months of Januaries IN A ROW.

All of the other months sound reasonably like their English equivalents, so no "images" will be given to help remember them.

English	Spanish	Pronounced
January	enero	ENERO
February	febrero	FEBRERO
March	marzo	MARTHO
April	abril	ABREEL
May	mayo	MAYO
June	junio	HOONEE O
July	julio	HOOLEE O
August	agosto	AGOSTO
September	setiembre	SETEE EMBRAY
October	octubre	OKTOOBRAY
November	noviembre	NOVEE EMBRAY
December	diciembre	DEETHEE EMBRAY

Now cover up the answers below and translate the following:

(You can write your answers in)

1. I AM ILL TODAY

2. GOODBYE; IT IS FEBRUARY; I AM SOON HERE

3. THE TOILETS ARE ENGAGED

4. I SPEAK QUIETLY; I LIVE QUIETLY; I SELL TELE-
   PHONES IN MARCH, IN APRIL AND IN SEPTEMBER

5. HE HAS A BAD MOUTH AND A BAD COUGH

The answers are:

1. ESTOY ENFERMO HOY

2. ADIÓS; ES FEBRERO; ESTOY PRONTO AQUÍ

3. LOS RETRETES ESTÁN OCUPADOS

4. HABLO TRANQUILAMENTE; VIVO TRANQUILA-
   MENTE; VENDO TELÉFONOS EN MARZO, EN ABRIL
   Y EN SETIEMBRE

5. TIENE UNA BOCA MALA Y UN TOS MALO

Now cover up the answers below and translate the following:

(You can write your answers in)

1. LA MUCHACHA Y LA MOSCA ESTABAN MUY ENFER-MAS EN ENERO
2. VENDO SILLAS, MESAS Y CAMAS EN MIS TIENDAS
3. SÍ, ESTÁ SUCIO, PERO ES MUY CARO
4. VENDO MUCHAS CEBOLLAS Y MUCHA CARNE
5. ¿DÓNDE ESTÁ EL PERRO HOY?

The answers are:

1. THE GIRL AND THE FLY WERE VERY ILL IN JANUARY
2. I SELL CHAIRS, TABLES AND BEDS IN MY SHOPS
3. YES, IT IS DIRTY, BUT IT IS VERY EXPENSIVE
4. I SELL MANY ONIONS AND MUCH MEAT
   (MUCHO in the plural — MUCHOS or MUCHAS — means MANY)
5. WHERE IS THE DOG TODAY?

A NUMBER OF USEFUL WORDS

THINK OF EACH IMAGE IN YOUR MIND'S EYE FOR ABOUT TEN SECONDS

○ The Spanish for SPECTACLES is (LAS) GAFAS   (GAFAS)
Imagine an Irishman saying "GIVE US my spectacles."

○ The Spanish for LEFT is IZQUIERDO   (EETHKEE ERDO)
Imagine thinking the driver in front
IS SCARED O' turning left.

○ The Spanish for RIGHT is DERECHO   (DERECHO)
Imagine asking if turning RIGHT will
lead you in the correct DIRECTION.

○ The Spanish for ENOUGH is BASTANTE   (BASTANTAY)
Imagine thinking "You've PASSED
AUNTIE ENOUGH sweets."

○ The Spanish for SERIOUS is GRAVE   (GRAVAY)
Imagine feeling GRAVE and SERIOUS.

○ The Spanish for TOWN is (LA) CIUDAD   (THEE OODAD)
Imagine pointing to a town and saying
"I'll SEE YOU THERE."

○ The Spanish for BUTTER is   (MANTEKEELYA)
MANTEQUILLA
Imagine your wife won't let you eat
butter, so you hire a MAN TO KILL HER.

○ The Spanish for TART is TARTA   (TARTA)
Imagine a bullfighter eating a TART.

○ The Spanish for GRAPE is UVA   (OOVA)
Imagine someone saying to you "HAVE A grape."

○ The Spanish for SALAD is ENSALADA   (ENSALADA)
Imagine being covered IN SALAD.

YOU CAN WRITE YOUR ANSWERS IN

○ What is the English for ensalada? _____

○ What is the English for uva? _____

○ What is the English for tarta? _____

○ What is the English for mantequilla? _____

○ What is the English for ciudad? _____

○ What is the English for grave? _____

○ What is the English for bastante? _____

○ What is the English for derecho? _____

○ What is the English for izquierdo? _____

○ What is the English for (las) gafas? _____

TURN BACK FOR THE ANSWERS

COVER UP THE LEFT HAND PAGE BEFORE ANSWERING

○ What is the Spanish for salad? _____

○ What is the Spanish for grape? _____

○ What is the Spanish for tart? _____

○ What is the Spanish for butter? _____

○ What is the Spanish for town? _____

○ What is the Spanish for serious? _____

○ What is the Spanish for enough? _____

○ What is the Spanish for right? _____

○ What is the Spanish for left? _____

○ What is the Spanish for spectacles? _____

TURN BACK FOR THE ANSWERS

SOME MORE USEFUL WORDS

THINK OF EACH IMAGE IN YOUR MIND'S EYE FOR ABOUT TEN SECONDS

○ The Spanish for CIGARETTE is (THEEGAREELYO)
CIGARILLO
Imagine Spanish cigarettes are like
little CIGARS that make you ILL OH!

○ The Spanish for BREAKFAST is (DESAYOONO)
DESAYUNO
Imagine someone coming up to you in
an hotel and saying "THEY SAY YOU
KNOW when breakfast is."

○ The Spanish for LUNCH is COMIDA (KOMEEDA)
Imagine lunch in your hotel is a
complete COMEDY of errors.

○ The Spanish for DINNER is CENA (THENA)
Imagine getting THINNER after eating your dinner.

○ The Spanish for TIP is PROPINA (PROPEENA)
Imagine PROPPING up a cup with your waiter's tip.

○ The Spanish for TOURIST is (EL) TURISTA (TOOREESTA)
Imagine a bullfighter talking to a group of TOURISTS.

○ The Spanish for TOBACCO is TABACO (TABAKO)
Imagine a bullfighter filling his pipe with TOBACCO.

○ The Spanish for NEWSPAPER is (PEREE ODEEKO)
PERIÓDICO
Imagine looking at your newspaper PERIODICALLY.

○ The Spanish for NAME is NOMBRE (NOMBRAY)
Imagine asking a policeman for his
name and NUMBER.

○ The Spanish for SOAP is JABÓN (HABON)
Imagine giving a child a piece of soap
and saying "HAVE ONE."

YOU CAN WRITE YOUR ANSWERS IN

○ What is the English for jabón? _____

○ What is the English for nombre? _____

○ What is the English for periódico? _____

○ What is the English for tabaco? _____

○ What is the English for (el) turista? _____

○ What is the English for propina? _____

○ What is the English for cena? _____

○ What is the English for comida? _____

○ What is the English for desayuno? _____

○ What is the English for cigarillo? _____

TURN BACK FOR THE ANSWERS

COVER UP THE LEFT HAND PAGE BEFORE ANSWERING

○ What is the Spanish for soap?   _____

○ What is the Spanish for name?   _____

○ What is the Spanish for newspaper?   _____

○ What is the Spanish for tobacco?   _____

○ What is the Spanish for tourist?   _____

○ What is the Spanish for tip?   _____

○ What is the Spanish for dinner?   _____

○ What is the Spanish for lunch?   _____

○ What is the Spanish for breakfast?   _____

○ What is the Spanish for cigarette?   _____

TURN BACK FOR THE ANSWERS

AND FINALLY, SOME MORE USEFUL WORDS

THINK OF EACH IMAGE IN YOUR MIND'S EYE FOR ABOUT TEN SECONDS

○ The Spanish for I GIVE is DOY   (DOY)
  Imagine thinking that I must GIVE My brother a
  TOY for his birthday.

○ The Spanish for I PUT is PONGO   (PONGO)
  Imagine thinking "If I PUT the deodorant here, it
  will make the PONG GO."

○ The Spanish for I GO is VOY   (VOY)
  Imagine thinking "I GO on a VOYage."

YOU CAN WRITE YOUR ANSWERS IN

○ What is the English for voy? _____

○ What is the English for pongo? _____

○ What is the English for doy? _____

TURN BACK FOR THE ANSWERS

YOU CAN WRITE YOUR ANSWERS IN

○ What is the Spanish for I go?   _____

○ What is the Spanish for I put?   _____

○ What is the Spanish for I give?   _____

TURN BACK FOR THE ANSWERS

Now cover up the answers below and translate the following:

(You can write your answers in)

1. I PUT THE SPECTACLES, THE BUTTER AND THE TART ON THE NEWSPAPER

2. I GIVE THE SOAP TODAY

3. I EAT THE BREAKFAST, THE SALAD AND THE LUNCH AND I EAT THE DINNER

4. I AM GOING THERE, AND THE TOURIST IS IN THE STREET

5. I WANT THE SOAP AND THE TOBACCO, BUT I DO NOT WANT A CIGARETTE AND I DO NOT WANT A TIP

The answers are:

1. PONGO LAS GAFAS, LA MANTEQUILLA Y LA TARTA EN EL PERIÓDICO

2. DOY EL JABÓN HOY

3. COMO EL DESAYUNO, LA ENSALADA Y LA COMIDA Y COMO LA CENA

4. VOY ALLÁ, Y EL TURISTA ESTÁ EN LA CALLE

5. QUIERO EL JABÓN Y EL TABACO, PERO NO QUIERO CIGARILLO Y NO QUIERO PROPINA

Now cover up the answers below and translate the following:

(You can write your answers in)

1. EL NOMBRE ESTÁ EN LA MANTEQUILLA Y EN LA CIUDAD
2. ESTOY TRANQUILO. ES OCTOBRE Y LA UVA ESTÁ EN LA TARTA
3. NO ES NOVIEMBRE. NO ES DICIEMBRE. NO ES AGOSTO. ES ENERO
4. VENDO EL PERIÓDICO EN MAYO, JUNIO Y JULIO
5. NO QUIERO EL JABÓN

The answers are:

1. THE NAME IS ON THE BUTTER AND IN THE TOWN
2. I AM QUIET. IT IS OCTOBER AND THE GRAPE IS IN THE TART
3. IT IS NOT NOVEMBER. IT IS NOT DECEMBER. IT IS NOT AUGUST. IT IS JANUARY
4. I SELL THE NEWSPAPER IN MAY, JUNE AND JULY
5. I DO NOT WANT THE SOAP

This is the end of the course. We hope you have enjoyed it! Of course words and grammar will not be remembered for ever without revision, but if you look at the book from time to time, you will be surprised at how quickly everything comes back.

When you go abroad, do not be too shy to try out what you have learnt. Your host will appreciate your making the effort to speak, even if you make mistakes. And the more you attempt to speak the more you will learn!

GLOSSARY

a (an)	un/una	but	pero
accident	accidente	butter	mantequilla
accountant	contador	cabbage	(la) col
afternoon	(la) tarde	cake	pastel
always	siempre	camping site	camping
am	estoy/soy	car	coche
ambulance	ambulancia	cat	gato
and	y	cauliflower	(la) coliflor
angry	enojado	chair	silla
animal	animal	cheap	barato
are	son/están	cheese	queso
arm	brazo	chemist's shop	farmacia
bad	malo	cheque	cheque
bandage	venda	chicken	pollo
bank	banco	cigarette	cigarillo
barber's shop	barbería	cloakroom	(el) guardarropa
bath	baño	clock	reloj
bathing trunks	bañador	coat	abrigo
beach	playa	coffee	café
bear	oso	cold	frío
bed	cama	colour	color
bedroom	dormitorio	cough	(la) tos
bee	abeja	cow	vaca
beer	cerveza	cup	taza
before	antes	cupboard	armario
bill	cuenta	curtain	cortina
bird	pájaro	customs	aduana
black	negro	danger	peligro
blood	(la) sangre	daughter	hija
blouse	blusa	day	(el) día
blue	azul	dead	muerto
boat	barco	deckchair	hamaca
book	libro	deep	profundo
boss	jefe	dentist	(el) dentista
bottle	botella	dining room	comedor
boy	muchacho	dinner	cena
bread	pan	dirty	sucio
breakfast	desayuno	doctor	médico
brother	hermano	dog	perro
bull	toro	donkey	burro
bullfight	corrida	door	puerta
bus	autobús	drawer	cajón
business	negocio	dress	vestido

driver	conductor	hat	sombrero
duck	pato	have (has)	tiene
easy	fácil	have (they)	tienen
eat (eats)	come	heat	calor
eat (they)	comen	hello	holá
egg	huevo	help	ayuda
elephant	elefante	her	su/sus
empty	vacío	here	aquí
engaged	ocupado	high	alto
engine	motor	his	su/sus
enough	bastante	holidays	(las) vacaciones
entrance	entrada	horse	caballo
envelope	sobre	hospital	hospital
exhaust	escape	hotel	hotel
exit	salida	hour	hora
expensive	caro	how	cómo
eye	ojo	how much	cuánto
face	cara	husband	marido
factory	fábrica	I eat	como
fan	ventilador	I give	doy
father	padre	I go	voy
fire	fuego	I have	tengo
first	primero	I live	vivo
fish	pez	I make	hago
floor	suelo	I put	pongo
flower	(la) flor	I sell	vendo
fly	mosca	I speak	hablo
fork	tenedor	I want	quiero
free	libre	ill	enfermo
fresh	fresco	in	en
friend	amigo	is	está/es
frog	rana	its	su/sus
fruit	fruta	jack	gato
garage	garage	jellyfish	medusa
garden	jardín	job	empleo
gentlemen	señores	key	(la) llave
girl	muchacha	kitchen	cocina
goat	cabra	knife	cuchillo
good	bueno	ladies	señoras
goodbye	adiós	lake	lago
goose	ganso	last	último
grape	uva	launderette	lavandería
green	verde	lawyer	abogado
grey	gris	left	izquierdo
hand	(la) mano	less	menos
hard	duro	letter	carta
hardware shop	ferretería	letter box	buzón

little	pequeño	piano	piano
long	largo	picnic	merienda
lunch	comida	pig	puerco
manager	director	plant	planta
map	(el) mapa	plate	plato
market	mercado	please	por favor
meat	(la) carne	police	policía
menu	menú	post office	correo
milk	(la) leche	potato	patata
minute	minuto	pretty	bonito
mirror	espejo	price	precio
mistake	error	product	producto
money	dinero	pump	bomba
monkey	mono	puncture	pinchazo
month	mes	quick	rápido
more	más	quickly	rápidamente
morning	mañana	quiet	tranquilo
mother	madre	quietly	tranquilamente
mountain	montana	rat	rata
mouse	ratón	receipt	recibo
mouth	boca	receptionist	recepcionista
much	mucho	red	rojo
museum	museo	rescue (to)	salvar
mushroom	seta	restaurant	restaurante
my	mi/mis	rice	arroz
name	nombre	right (correct)	correcto
newspaper	periódico	right	derecho
night	(la) noche	river	río
no/not	no	road	carretera
number	número	rock	roca
office	oficina	room	(la) habitación
oil	aceite	salad	ensalada
old	viejo	salary	salario
on	en	salesman	vendedor
onion	cebolla	salmon	salmón
only	solamente	sand	arena
or	o	sea	mar
outside	fuera de	seat	asiento
owner	propietario	second (adj)	segundo
pain	dolor	second	segundo
paper	papel	serious	grave
party	fiesta	shelf	estante
passport	pasaporte	shirt	camisa
path	senda	shoe	zapato
pear	pera	shop	tienda
pen	pluma	sir	señor
petrol	gasolina	sister	hermana

251

skin	(la) piel	was	estaba
skirt	falda	wasp	avispa
soap	jabón	week	semana
some	unos/unas	were	estaban
son	hijo	wheel	rueda
soon	pronto	where	dónde
sorry	perdone	white	blanco
soup	sopa	who	quién
spectacles	(las) gafas	why	por qué
stairs	escalera	wife	mujer
stamp	sello	window	ventana
storm	tormenta	wine	vino
sugar	azúcar	wrong	incorrecto
suitcase	maleta	year	ano
sun	sol	yellow	amarillo
supermarket	supermercado	yes	sí
table	mesa	yesterday	ayer
tablecloth	mantel	your	su/sus
tank (petrol)	depósito		
tart	tarta		
telephone	teléfono		
thank you	gracias		
the (plural)	los/las	**Days of the week**	
the	el/la	Monday	lunes
there	allá	Tuesday	martes
thief	ladrón	Wednesday	miércoles
thing	cosa	Thursday	jueves
ticket	billete	Friday	viernes
time	tiempo	Saturday	sábado
tip	propina	Sunday	domingo
tobacco	tobaco		
tobacconist	tabaquería		
today	hoy		
toilet	retrete		
tomato	tomate	**Months of the Year**	
tourist	(el) turista	January	enero
town	(la) ciudad	February	febrero
train	tren	March	marzo
tree	árbol	April	abril
trousers	pantalones	May	mayo
tyre	neumático	June	junio
under	debajo de	July	julio
very	muy	August	agosto
waitress	camarera	September	setiembre
wall	(la) pared	October	octubre
want (they)	quieren	November	noviembre
want (wants)	quiere	December	diciembre

252

Numbers

zero	cero	eight	ocho
one	uno	nine	nueve
two	dos	ten	diez
three	tres	eleven	once
four	cuatro	twelve	doce
five	cinco	twenty	veinte
six	seis	twenty-five	veinticinco
seven	siete	quarter	cuarto
		half	media

LINKWORD
LANGUAGE SYSTEM

The fastest, the easiest, the most enjoyable way to learn a language!

Pick up 400 words and basic grammar in just 12 hours with LINKWORD

* Travelling * Eating Out * Telling the Time * Emergencies * At the Hotel * Going Shopping * Numbers * Clothes * Family * On the Beach

Ideal for holidays, business travel, schoolwork

'Unforgettable memory joggers'
The Sunday Times

'It took 12 hours to teach a regime that normally takes 40 hours'
Training manager, Thomson Holidays

'It works and it's fun'
Guardian

Available for the following languages

0 552 130532 FRENCH
0 552 130559 SPANISH
0 552 139068 PORTUGUESE
0 552 139165 FURTHER FRENCH

0 552 130540 GERMAN
0 552 130567 ITALIAN
0 552 139076 GREEK

LINKWORD
ON COMPUTER

by Dr Michael M. Gruneberg

First Courses
* FRENCH * GERMAN * SPANISH * ITALIAN * GREEK
* RUSSIAN * DUTCH * PORTUGUESE

On IBM PC & COMPATIBLES, APPLE II Series and BBC Model
(B) disk only.
*Also available on MACINTOSH and COMMODORE 64 (USA
only).

GCSE LEVEL FRENCH

An extensive vocabulary and grammar up to GCSE level standard,
ideal as a follow-up course to the book or first course programs or as a
revision or 'brush-up' course for the rusty!

Available on IBM PC & Compatibles.

For further information please contact:

MINERVA SOFTWARE,
MINERVA HOUSE,
BARING CRESCENT,
EXETER.
EX1 1TL
TEL: (0392) 437756

ARTWORK INC.,
1844 PENFIELD ROAD,
PENFIELD,
NEW YORK
TEL: (716) 385 6120

LINKWORD
AUDIO TAPES

An audio tape is available as an extra learning aid to accompany this book.

It allows you to hear and to practise the correct pronunciation for all the words used on this course.

The tape is available by mail order using the order form at the back of this book.

Other LINKWORD AUDIO TAPES:

0 552 13225X FRENCH   0 552 132268 GERMAN
0 552 132276 SPANISH   0 552 132284 ITALIAN
0 552 139661 PORTUGUESE   0 552 139556 GREEK

LINKWORD
BOOK AND AUDIO TAPE PACKS

The following LINKWORD courses are also available in packs combining the books with the relevant pronunciation cassette tape.

These are available either by mail order, using the form at the back of this book, or you can buy the pack from any good bookshop:

0 552 005002 FRENCH   **0 552 005010 SPANISH**
0 552 003700 GERMAN

LINKWORD LANGUAGE SYSTEM BOOKS, AUDIO TAPES AND BOOK AND TAPE PACKS AVAILABLE FROM CORGI BOOKS

THE PRICES SHOWN BELOW WERE CORRECT AT THE TIME OF GOING TO PRESS. HOWEVER TRANSWORLD PUBLISHERS RESERVE THE RIGHT TO SHOW NEW RETAIL PRICES ON COVERS WHICH MAY DIFFER FROM THOSE PREVIOUSLY ADVERTISED IN THE TEXT OR ELSEWHERE.

☐	13053 2	LINKWORD LANGUAGE SYSTEM: FRENCH	£4.99
☐	13054 0	LINKWORD LANGUAGE SYSTEM: GERMAN	£4.99
☐	13055 9	LINKWORD LANGUAGE SYSTEM: SPANISH	£4.99
☐	13056 7	LINKWORD LANGUAGE SYSTEM: ITALIAN	£4.99
☐	13907 6	LINKWORD LANGUAGE SYSTEM: GREEK	£4.99
☐	13906 8	LINKWORD LANGUAGE SYSTEM: PORTUGUESE	£4.99
☐	13916 5	LINKWORD LANGUAGE SYSTEM: FURTHER FRENCH	£4.99
☐	13225 X	LINKWORD AUDIO TAPE: FRENCH	£6.95
☐	13226 8	LINKWORD AUDIO TAPE: GERMAN	£6.95
☐	13227 6	LINKWORD AUDIO TAPE: SPANISH	£6.95
☐	13228 4	LINKWORD AUDIO TAPE: ITALIAN	£6.95
☐	13955 6	LINKWORD AUDIO TAPE: GREEK	£6.95
☐	13966 1	LINKWORD AUDIO TAPE: PORTUGUESE	£6.95
☐	00500 2	LINKWORD BOOK AND TAPE PACK: FRENCH*	£10.99
☐	00501 0	LINKWORD BOOK AND TAPE PACK: SPANISH*	£11.99
☐	00370 0	LINKWORD BOOK AND TAPE PACK: GERMAN*	£11.99

*inclusive of VAT

All Corgi/Bantam Books are available at your bookshop or newsagent, or can be ordered from the following address:
Corgi/Bantam Books,
Cash Sales Department,
P.O. Box 11, Falmouth, Cornwall TR10 9EN

UK and B.F.P.O. customers please send a cheque or postal order (no currency) and allow £1.00 for postage and packing for the first book plus 50p for the second book and 30p for each additional book to a maximum charge of £3.00 (7 books plus).

Overseas customers, including Eire, please allow £2.00 for postage and packing for the first book plus £1.00 for the second book and 50p for each subsequent title ordered.

NAME (Block Letters) ....

ADDRESS ....

....